THE SECRETARY OF STATE

THE SECRETARY OF STATE

by

DAVID KYNASTON

Offices of State
Series Editor: M. M. Reese

TERENCE DALTON
LAVENHAM . SUFFOLK
1978

Published by
TERENCE DALTON LIMITED
ISBN 0 900963 80 8

Text photoset in 11/13pt Baskerville

Printed in Great Britain at
THE LAVENHAM PRESS LIMITED
LAVENHAM   .   SUFFOLK

Contents

Index of Illustrations

To my parents

General Introduction

T HE British have great respect for their ancient institutions without perhaps knowing very much about them; and it is a strange fact that, so far, the knowledge has never been easily accessible in a simple and compact form likely to attract readers interested in their origins and historical development.

Thus the publisher, Terence Dalton, has had the excellent idea of projecting a series of short books on the great Offices of State, or the officers who fill them. The books are as accurate as it has been possible to make them, having regard to the uncertainty and controversy that surround the early origins. English constitutional development has been notoriously haphazard, and in certain areas it is impossible to go beyond conjecture. But where the great offices have suddenly taken long strides or moved in new directions, this has usually been due to statesmen of outstanding calibre or determination. The authors' recognition of the quirks and accomplishments of these famous men brings a personal flavour to the narrative and reminds us that constitutional progress has seldom been achieved without passion and struggle.

The Secretary of State is one of the first two titles introducing this series. The author, David Kynaston, is a young Oxford scholar whose thorough examination of the evidence has set up some interesting new perspectives. His book should be of value not only to specialists and students but to all readers who wish to understand more about the State that now bulks so large in everyone's life.

M. M. Reese,
Hindhead,
December 1977

Preface

GEORGE II aroused much popular hostility when he dismissed the elder Pitt in April 1757 and a notice was attached to the portals of St James's Palace which read: "A Secretary of State wanted; much honesty not necessary; no principle will be treated with". Yet two centuries later, following the various sub-divisions of the secretaryship, the fact of the office barely registers in the popular or even perhaps the scholarly consciousness. Writing about Stanley Ayling's recent biography of the elder Pitt, reviewers almost without exception referred to Pitt in 1756 becoming War Minister, a non-existent position, not Secretary of State. Such an oversight is a pity: the secretaryship before 1782 was rarely other than an interesting office and many of the individual Secretaries deserve to be rescued from that obscurity which one might term as the typing-pool of history.

For my material I am largely dependent on the researches of others. The bibliography will reveal my more major debts. I have concentrated in the text almost exclusively on the office and its holders, with the result that much of the detail concerning the political and diplomatic circumstances of the day is only alluded to or even ignored. In a book of this length covering a period of over four hundred years there seemed no alternative. Nor with such diffuse subject matter to be covered did I find it possible to avoid the "narrative" and "analysis" breakdown that I have adopted for the post-Cromwell chapters. And, indeed, it is truly said that though history may never be less than biography, it must always be something more. The problem rather is to avoid the formalised strait-jacket that at one time tended to characterise administrative studies. Ultimately power counts, not the trappings: it is the attempt by a succession of "new men" to fulfil this pragmatic dictum that lends the history of the secretaryship its peculiar significance.

My thanks to Max Reese for sympathetic editing and to Penry Williams and Nicholas Underhill for helpful discussions about the earlier part of the period. The responsibility remains mine for errors and infelicities.

Note: For Secretaries who change names I have adopted in the text the name by which they were most commonly known while Secretary. Thus: William Cecil (but Burghley where appropriate in order to differentiate him from his son), Robert Cecil, Arlington, Harley, St John, and Carteret.

CHAPTER ONE

KING'S SECRETARIES: 1377-1534

1377-81: Robert Braybrook
1381-5: John Bacon
1385-7: Richard Medford
1393-5: Roger Walden
1395-9: John Lincoln
1402: Nicholas Bubbewith
1402-6: John Prophet
1406-13: William Pilton
1412: Richard Holme
1413-19: John Stone
1419-20: William Hayton
1420: Richard Cowdray
1421-2: William Alnwick
1422: John Stopyndon
1430-2: William Hayton
1437-43: Thomas Beckington

1443-55: Richard Andrew
1443: William Toly
1455-60: Thomas Manning
1460: James Goldwell
1462-5: John Bothe
1466-80: William Hatteclyffe
1470; 1472-4: Peter Courtenay
1474: William Slefeld
1480-3: Oliver King
1483-5: John Kendall
1485-7: Richard Fox
1487-95: Oliver King
1495-1500: Robert Sherborne
1500-16: Thomas Ruthal
1516-26: Richard Pace
1526-9: William Knight
1529-34: Stephen Gardiner

CHAPTER ONE

The King's Secretary: 1377-1534

"The name of Secretary hath the foundation upon the knowledge of such things as ought to be kept secret".

THESE words of Sir Robert Wingfield in June 1516, criticising the recent appointment of Richard Pace as the King's Secretary, were historically shrewd, unfair though they were to Pace himself, a discreet enough figure. At least up to the fourteenth century a "secretarius" of the king was essentially a secret agent, as likely as not engaged in diplomatic activities. Such a man, however, was not a member of the royal secretariat in the sense of writing and dispatching documents. For these functional origins of the modern Secretary of State one must go back to the Normans. Although tenth-century kings, from the reign of Athelstan (925-40) at the latest, had granted charters and thus created some sort of writing office, it was not until after 1066 that the number of writs and charters began to proliferate; and the chancellor, and below him the clerics in the expanding chancery, administered and recorded this royal business. Gradually over the course of the next century, however, the chancellor developed in capacity from being merely the passive recorder of the king's will, ceased indeed to be secretarial in an intimate sense, and instead emerged as the first great officer of state, no longer necessarily accountable only to the king himself. The process may best be characterised as one of "going public"; and it anticipated what would subsequently become a

1

familiar bureaucratic pattern amongst the leading executive aides of the medieval monarchy.

The decisive reign was that of Henry II, a king who enjoyed business and significantly expanded the scope of government. In consequence, the chancellor was no longer able to spend all his time hovering round the king's person, waiting to perform his master's will. The developing role of the great seal revealed the implications of this changing situation. Introduced under continental influence in the eleventh century to replace cross-making as the regular means of validating royal documents, the great seal now accompanied its keeper, the chancellor, out of court, with the result that by the thirteenth century a king who wished to impose himself on the administrative process was beginning to have to look elsewhere for the legal instrument with which to do so. The means chosen for this purpose proved to be the privy seal, the very name suggesting a return to the royal personage. Suitably, it seems first to have manifested itself as an alternative seal under King John, a monarch looking for firm royal action. Yet in the event it never quite fulfilled its early promise. It failed to develop an office of its own and the king's writing clerks continued to be chancery men; the barons naturally mistrusted the seal and sought to keep it under the check of the council; while the actual keepers of the privy seal, though continuing for some time to perform secretarial duties on behalf of their monarchs, nevertheless became increasingly public-minded figures during the fourteenth century. The last man to combine the roles of private secretary and public statesman was William of Wykeham, who in 1367 surrendered the keepership of the privy seal in order to become chancellor. Once again a new structure was needed if personal royal authority was not to become meaningless.

This time the guardian of that authority was to be the King's Secretary proper; and the seal in his charge was to be the signet, the 'fifth in a series of secret seals initiated by Edward II in 1314 as a way of counteracting his growing loss of control over the privy seal. The secret seal did disappear in the early part of Edward III's reign, but re-emerged again towards the end of his minority. Pope Urban V acknowledged the seal's significance when he wrote to Edward III in August 1363 in response to a royal request: "As the pope sees by the king's secret seal that he has the matter much at heart, he will grant the request if possible". The one-inch secret seal vied for a time with the smaller signet version, but by the end of Edward III's reign was no longer in use. The status of the signet seal as the king's private seal was confirmed in 1377 when on his accession the child Richard II was given a formal keeper, to be called the King's Secretary, to look after it. These were intimate beginnings and foreshadowed the supremely flexible influence that the office was eventually to exercise.

The Early Secretaries: 1377-99

The fact that during the first three weeks of the reign the signet was used not only as such but also instead of the privy seal, while a new privy seal was being made, showed the extent to which the development of the secretaryship was essentially administrative in purpose, a question of getting work done that necessarily involved some degree of royal participation. The first keeper of the signet and thus King's Secretary was Robert Braybrook, a trained lawyer of Northamptonshire gentry background who received an *honorarium* of around £25 a year for his labours. Twice during his secretaryship he went on diplomatic missions abroad, resulting in a personal loss to himself of some £70. The second of these was an important one, to Bruges in the early months of 1381 to negotiate with Bohemian representatives about the proposed marriage of Richard to Anne of Bohemia, but significantly Braybrook was accompanied by four other envoys, among whom he was not the most senior. Indeed, continuity and moderation seem to have been the keynotes of his secretaryship. Only very few signet warrants as yet missed out the privy seal stage before going to chancery and being issued under the great seal; while in terms of quantity, it is a striking fact that among the chancery warrants one signet file alone covers the period from 1377 to 1383, in contrast to the sixteen files that represent the six-year period after 1383. But these later developments, with their political connotations, were after Braybrook's time. By September 1381 he had become bishop of London, in which capacity the criticisms he earned for his lack of stringency in dealing with the prostitute problem were mild compared to the tribulations suffered by his immediate secretarial successors.

Signs of opposition to an increasingly coherent royal party first became apparent during the secretaryship (1381-5) of John Bacon, who had come up through the royal household and in March 1385 resigned his position to become ambassador to Pope Urban VI. Later in the year he died abroad and Richard made a point of attending the mass for his soul at Westminster. His successor as Secretary was Richard Medford, formerly a clerk in Richard's private chapel. He now more than ever stayed close to the king, took up Bacon's work in the development of an organised signet office, and was clearly a prime victim of Chancellor Arundel's resolution in October 1386 no longer to accept the signet as sufficient authority for the deployment of the great seal. The bold attempt by an adolescent king and his circle to implement personal rule now met its match in the resolute opposition of the lords appellant. Medford's fate mirrored that of his royal master: decline, followed by a relative revival. 1387 was spent by Medford accompanying Richard on his desperate attempt to rally support in the provinces. Then came a spell in the Tower from Christmas 1387 to June 1388, followed by release on bail and, in 1390, a bishopric. Neither the signet seal nor the secretaryship itself, however, was rehabilitated so quickly. The Merciless Parliament of 1388 reiterated the determination of the lords appellant two years earlier not to permit signet warrants for chancery purposes; and between 1388 and 1392 nothing is heard in any formal sense of the office of the King's Secretary. Yet out of the extremes of the 1380s there did emerge in the 1390s a working arrangement concerning the seals which effectively laid the foundations for the slow but fairly sure development of the fifteenth-century Secretary.

The first major indication of compromise came in January 1390 when Parliament successfully petitioned Richard that in future the keeper of the privy seal must not be by-passed when signet letters of pardon were sent to chancery. In effect this offered some sort of bulwark against too-direct royal action in return for an acceptance of the signet as part of the normal sealing process. Gradually a certain balance was established. The signature of John Macclesfield is to be seen on various signet letters between February 1390 and January 1393, but he does not appear to have become Secretary. Roger Walden, however, did, probably early in 1393, after several years as treasurer of Calais, during which time he distinguished himself by taking part in 1388 on a stirring cattle raid into French lands. Walden was an incisive character who later in the 1390s became archbishop of Canterbury, though as a contemporary admitted he was "better versed in things of the camp and the world than of the church and the study". In October 1394 Walden went with Richard to Ireland, where for want of an alternative secretariat he reconstructed and enlarged what was in effect a mobile signet office. To do this he drew heavily on the experience of not only Medford (now treasurer of Ireland as well as bishop of Chichester), but also John Lincoln of Grimsby, who had been active in the royal circle in the mid-1380s and subsequently shared imprisonment with Medford. All the evidence about Lincoln suggests a man of considerable ability. In February 1395 he was probably responsible for a lucid paper expounding for the benefit of the council at Westminster the important distinctions between "Irrois savages nos enemis, Irrois rebels et Engleis obeissantz"; and later in the year, in October, Lincoln succeeded Walden to the secretaryship, with Walden himself becoming treasurer. The omens seemed to point only one way — yet this time the political rupture of 1386 was not to be repeated.

The explanation for this fulfilment of the tacit compromise of 1390 lay in the general acceptance of the constitutional principle that the efficient working of the signet was indispensable to any reasonable exercise of royal authority. Behind the compact was the reformed behaviour of Richard himself. First in Ireland he employed the signet for household rather than chancery purposes; and later back in England, even after the full restoration of his power in 1397, he overtly refrained from expanding the signet's use. Lincoln meanwhile continued to build up the signet office, recruiting up to three clerks of the signet, two of whom may even have received pensions. The bi-partisan role of the signet during the course of Richard's fall in 1399 confirmed its new acceptability. In front of the assembled magnates at Westminster, and aware of the need to cede gracefully, Richard turned to his expectant successor, Henry of Lancaster, and "as a sign of his intention and wish in the matter, took the ring of gold of his patent signet from his finger, and put it on the finger of the duke". Henry for his part, having claimed the throne and been acknowledged king, solemnly displayed the signet as symbol of his rightful accession. Constitutionally the signet had come to stay.

Fifteenth-Century Secretaries

The fifteenth century in many ways set the tone for the future of secretarial history. At the more subterranean level, that of the governmental use of the signet and the accompanying growth of the signet office, forerunner of the modern secretariat, there was relatively steady progress, though not without some ups and downs; while at the higher level of actual office-holding all was dependent upon chance and circumstance, above all the nature of royal authority and the character of the King's Secretary. Right at the outset the lack of cut-and-dried definition is apparent. We know that Lincoln survived personally in 1399, but had to give up the secretaryship. Apart from that, however, there is no clear evidence concerning the keeper of the signet between 1399 and 1402, though at one point Henry IV does refer to Thomas Langley, later his chancellor, as "nosterus Secretaire". The first two Secretaries of the reign one can be sure of were Nicholas Bubbewith in 1402 and John Prophet between 1402 and 1406. Both were career men who used the secretaryship as convenient stepping-stones. Bubbewith had been a king's clerk and a master of chancery and was to become keeper of the rolls, keeper of the privy seal, and in due course treasurer. Prophet's history was not dissimilar: by 1386 he was a king's clerk, by the 1390s the first salaried clerk of the council, while as Secretary he attempted to combine close attendance upon the itinerant Henry with getting to the council at Westminster whenever he could. In 1406 he gave up the secretaryship to become keeper of the privy seal. The date is significant, for in that year, after this short period of capable secretaryship clearly to Henry's liking, the lords of the council turned the screws on the king, who for the rest of his reign seems only rarely to have exercised any personal influence on the letters coming out of the signet office. The Secretary in this last phase was William Pilton, about whom little is known apart from the fact that he was a familiar type of clerical prebend-collector who in 1412 secured a life's dispensation from residence. It is possible that also in 1412 Richard Holme, a long-standing king's clerk with some diplomatic experience, was appointed as a second Secretary. If this was so, it not only anticipated the practice that was to become common the following century, but it also showed how there could develop a measure of growth and planned continuity in the secretarial office even during a relatively obscure phase. The king had to be attended upon, and signet letters still had to be written, even though for the time being the work may not have been of the highest moment.

Secretary from 1413 until his death in May 1419 was John Stone, who in the usual way had come up from being a king's clerk. Henry V's proved to be a good reign for the signet: the king was often away campaigning in France, from where he used signet letters both to supervise his military resources and also to address frequent instructions to the council at home. From the time of his invasion in 1415 these letters were written no longer in French, but instead in English. Significantly, as perhaps befitted a king with considerable personal will-power, Henry did not always extend his full trust to Stone. A letter of 1417 concerned with high diplomacy ended: "For the secretness of this matter, I have written this instruction with my own hand, and sealed it with my signet of the eagle". The death of Stone himself signalled three years of rapid turn-over. William Hayton, formerly a clerk of the signet and probably appointed a few weeks before Stone actually died, only stayed in office until 1420. Also in 1420 the diplomatist Richard Cowdray had a short spell as Secretary. He was succeeded from 1421 to 1422 by William Alnwick, who was confessor to both Henry V and the young Henry VI and later in the 1420s became keeper of the privy seal. A certain John Stopyndon seems also to have overlapped for a while as Secretary during 1422. In the same year, however, Henry V died of dysentery and Henry VI came to the throne aged nine months. No Secretary seems to have been considered necessary. One was appointed (William Hayton, perhaps the same man as before) to attend the king in France in the early 1430s; but on the royal return in 1432 the duke of Gloucester, the king's uncle, dismissed five household officers, including Hayton, and named only four replacements. If the king was to remain a puppet, there was still no point in giving him a Secretary.

Around 1437, however, things changed. Henry began to seek to impose himself; and in Thomas Beckington he found a Secretary of thoroughbred quality. Beckington was a man of considerable learning and had been a legal adviser to Archbishop Chichele in the court of Canterbury and also chancellor to the duke of Gloucester, a notable patron of the emerging generation of English humanist scholars. After his secretaryship (1437-43) Beckington continued to flourish. Following a few months as lord privy seal he was consecrated by Alnwick late in 1443 to the see of Bath and Wells. Fittingly the ceremony took place at Eton College, which Beckington had recently helped to found. He seems to have been a wise bishop and particularly left his mark on Wells as a builder. All of this suggests that Beckington was a great man, the first of comparable calibre to hold the secretarial office for any length of time. As Secretary he reorganised the signet office, introduced a much clearer, less traditionally scholastic style of Latin into the Italian diplomatic correspondence, and is reputed to have attended on Henry as his reader almost every day. Twice, however, he went abroad on diplomatic business. On the first mission, accompanying Cardinal Beaufort to Calais in 1439 in an effort to obtain peace terms from the French king, Beckington experienced what was to become a familiar secretarial plight. He wrote to a friend in August: "Whatever I did, whether eating, drinking or sleeping, I was tormented in spirit, and the thoughts of my heart were always occupied with what was going on at home". Three years later Beckington again had a difficult time when with two other household officers he set off for the court of Armagnac in order to secure one of the daughters of the count as a wife for Henry. They reached Bordeaux, but found it threatened, and Beckington recorded in his journal on 10th August: "Today being the feast of Saint Lawrence, the following letter was sent to the king, with the utmost secrecy of conveyance, by an old pilgrim. It was written in three lines, on vellum, the whole length of the skin, and was sewed up in the border of his garment". In the event the mission proved literally a freeze-out. The military situation deteriorated steadily and the winter became so bad that the artist commissioned to paint the portraits of the three daughters for Henry's scrutiny was only able to complete one before his colours solidified. Beckington was home by February 1443, doubtless thankfully, and a few months afterwards gave up the secretaryship.

It is tempting to see Beckington's influence behind the various council ordinances that were issued between 1440 and 1444 and together sought to make indispensable the role of the signet and thus by definition diminish the importance of the privy seal, which during Henry's minority had become increasingly identified with the barons who dominated the council. The key regulation of 1444 about the granting of bills and letters under the signet was worded as follows: "Then the king's goodness, if it pleases him, shall put thereto his hand, and sign the bill immediately after the said writing. Or he shall command his chamberlain to subscribe it, or take it to his Secretary, commanding him to do this. So that, from the time when it is signed in the manner and form above said, no man shall add to it or take away from it". It is possible to argue that this regulation—making the signet and Secretary central to the warrant-making process—was the first and most decisive step on the road towards making the Secretary one of the great "public" officers of state. But this ignores too much the context of the time: Henry was seeking to assert himself and he clearly realised that the instrument which would serve his purposes best was the signet. For three more centuries at least Secretaries were to operate within the political framework of a succession of monarchs of varying impulse and ability in terms of trying to impose their will on their leading subjects. By 1444 Henry VI had the opportunity to be the real king that he was expected to be. But he wasted the chance, and his Secretaries suffered accordingly.

The evidence does not allow an exact chronology, but it is probable that the use of the signet held fairly steady until 1453, when Henry went mad for the first time and the exercise of this seal went into a steep decline. Moreover, under the auspices of the conciliar-minded dukes of Somerset and York the privy seal once again reasserted itself. Henry's Secretary from 1443 to 1455 was Richard Andrew, a yeoman's son and another Chichele protégé, who came to the office after five years as the first warden of All Souls. Andrew may have shared the position early on with William Toly, a former signet clerk, but though he emerged as the sole Secretary he does not seem to have been a dominant figure. Certainly his royal master's weaknesses did not help, nor the fact that he was several times away as an envoy negotiating in Scotland. Andrew's successor was Thomas Manning, described in 1458 as "vir solidus, sobrius, et sensatus". In 1460, however, Manning resigned, apparently because of ill-health, to be succeeded for an indeterminate period by James Goldwell, who was later in the 1460s to become Edward IV's orator at the Roman Curia. Manning, meanwhile had not ended his troubles merely by resigning his office. In 1461 he

was attainted following the fall of Henry and in 1465 was captured
with Henry near Bungerly Hippingstones in Lancashire. Soon afterwards he was released from the Tower, "aged and infected with a
white leper", and in 1469 died in penury. It was a salutary tale.
Though subsequently pensions, sinecures, and a measure of liberal
decency did to some extent protect the personal fates of most
Secretaries against whom the political winds blew, the essence of the
situation, inextricably one of "ins" and "outs", was not to change. The
secretarial tenure, and the reputation of the occupant himself,
remained perhaps more than any other office uninsurable.

At this stage, following the Wars of the Roses, a strong dose of
personal monarchy was clearly needed—and Edward IV willingly
provided it. The secretarial history of the reign is nevertheless
somewhat confusing, for Edward liked to employ his Secretaries as
diplomatists, and for that reason twice resorted to the double-
secretaryship device, enabling one to stay at home and conduct the
signet correspondence while the other was abroad. Secretary from
1462 until 1465, when he became bishop of Exeter, was John Bothe,
who during his secretaryship also nominally held the post of chancellor
of Cambridge University. He was succeeded, probably in 1466, by
William Hatteclyffe, who held the office until 1480. Two of his fellow-
Secretaries during this span were Peter Courtenay, in December 1470
(during Henry VI's short-lived return to the throne) and from 1472 to
1474, and William Slefeld, during 1474. Courtenay was evidently an
able man who had already done diplomatic work for Edward in the
1460s and was to become bishop of Exeter in 1478. All that is known
about Slefeld is that he was very active diplomatically in the 1470s.
The central secretarial figure, however, is Hatteclyffe himself.
Early in his career he had been physician to Queen Margaret and had
helped to care for Henry during his madness. But his allegiance was
Yorkist and in 1461, following the second Battle of St Albans and with
Margaret still posing a threat to the security of London, Hatteclyffe
was one of the party who, under orders from the duchess of York, set
out for Ireland with royal treasure in their protection. A French boat
captured them, however, and they were only released upon payment of
a heavy ransom. Edward subsequently gave Hatteclyffe £40 as com-
pensation for the ordeal. As Secretary, Hatteclyffe had a similarly

mixed experience, quite apart from his period of imprisonment during Henry's restoration. Although abroad so often on diplomatic missions that he clearly fulfilled his master's expectations of him, nevertheless the fact of Hatteclyffe's frequent absences undoubtedly checked the progress in the stature of the secretarial office, in spite of Edward's considerably increased use of the signet during the 1470s. "I shall abide still where the king shall be at all times", Hatteclyffe asserted in 1474, but it was not to be. And indeed, early in 1480, shortly before his death, another fellow-Secretary was appointed to assist him, although on this occasion to look after the signet as much on account of Hatteclyffe's absences through age as through diplomatic duties. This "co-adjutor", as he was called, was Oliver King, who soon became sole Secretary and as such embodied in the office for the first time a fairly precise bureaucratic structure, albeit within a strictly "personal" household context.

King's background was revealing: between 1473 and 1475 he had been a clerk of the signet and during the decade as a whole had been sent on several diplomatic missions to France. When Edward IV died in April 1483 he stayed in office as Secretary during the short minority of Edward V, in notable contrast to the precedent of some sixty years earlier. Richard III, however, not unexpectedly sent him to the Tower and replaced him with John Kendall, who had been his secretary when he was duke of Gloucester. Kendall's successor after Bosworth (where he was probably killed) was Richard Fox, Secretary for two years only and moving on in 1487 to become lord privy seal and eventually, in 1501, bishop of Winchester. Fox's career indicates that the status of the secretaryship was not yet exalted enough for the position to be held by first-rank intimates of the king, though after King returned as Secretary in 1487 the office seems to have grown in prestige. Henry VII, writing to the Pope in 1490, noted how King was "always in attendance on our person". Moreover, when made bishop of Exeter in 1492, King did what none of his predecessors had done in a similar circumstance, which was to continue as Secretary. In fact he never entered the diocese and was only to give up the secretaryship on being promoted in 1495 to the see of Bath and Wells. Undoubtedly King's decision of 1492 represented a certain turning-point: the Secretary may not yet in a functional sense have particularly expanded his scope,

but at least when the right conjunction of king, servant, and circumstance did come along it would be conceptually possible, if still
somewhat disturbing to conservative minds, for the personal agent to
be transformed into a Crown minister.

Pre-Tudor Development

King's decision also represents a good point for some sort of
fifteenth-century secretarial stock-taking. To go further into the
question of status: formal privilege is always difficult to evaluate in
comparison with informal esteem, but it was probably significant that
it was Beckington who became the first Secretary to receive cloth from
the great wardrobe as well as the usual secretarial writing accessories.
Other evidence comes from the various extant household ordinances.
One of 1454 shows the Secretary above the chaplains in rank, but
below the knights; another of 1478 puts the Secretary on a par with the
almoners, the cofferer, and the dean of the chapel, though at the same
time assigns to the chamberlain a distinct and more nourishing mess.
For their income the Secretaries of the period depended upon a
mixture of fees received for making out signet letters, gratuities from
interested parties seeking the attention of king or council, and various
benefices that came their way. Though the age of the clerical
administrator was on the wane, only two of the fifteenth-century
Secretaries were in fact laymen, these exceptions being Hatteclyffe and
Kendall. The Secretaries were educated men, usually graduates, often
with a law degree. In terms of social background, they seem, as
befitted a new office, to have been drawn on the whole from the
smaller gentry, though there were even humbler exceptions like
Andrew, Fox, and most notably Beckington. These were indeed "new
men", representatives of a type whose main chance would come soon.

Turning to the instrument the Secretaries controlled, the signet, it
was not until the reign of Henry VII, who took the policy of Edward IV
to its logical extension, that the smaller seal really began to dominate
the privy seal. Though the exchequer continued to insist on specific
authorisation from the privy seal before it acted, and of course any
positive decisions that involved the council still necessarily involved the
use of the privy seal, nevertheless the growth in the use of the signet
under Henry VII was remarkably rapid. But here one must differen-

tiate: some signet warrants, like those considered in the regulations of the early 1440s, were of the formal type that went to chancery via the privy seal, and the crucial question concerning these was whether or not they were interfered with on the way; while others either went direct to chancery or were even issued without reference to the other two seals at all. The particular contribution of Edward IV and Henry VII was to increase greatly the use of the more immediate type of signet warrants and in addition bring out their potential administrative usage as well as their more traditional personal royal purpose. Edward IV, the first king to begin in a systematic way to attach his own sign manual to signet letters, addressed a not untypical instruction through this form when he told his council to make sure that the local dignitaries of Coventry did not interfere with one of his servants, a certain John French, who was seeking to practise the art of transmuting metals. Personal monarchy clearly meant something when it was applied at this level. Yet one can easily exaggerate: the signet remained essentially the king's personal seal and only assumed its new importance because of the personal qualities of Edward IV and Henry VII, an importance which it substantially lost during the period of Wolsey's firm chancellorship. And when the Secretary did evolve into a true officer of state, this was to be a development only marginally related to the fortunes of the various seals, which were essentially a medieval phenomenon.

The fifteenth-century signet office followed the same pattern as the signet itself: nascently bureaucratic, but still at base a household institution. It tended to consist, besides the Secretary, of four senior clerks, with perhaps three junior clerks under them. Though still more often called the office of the King's Secretary rather than the signet office, the fact that it began from the first half of the century to keep records of its activities suggests that the formalising process was under way. Nevertheless, the clerks of the signet seem in a professional sense to have had a far more difficult and ambivalent existence than their counterparts of the privy seal, who at least enjoyed the facilities of a distinctive *hospicium* in which to operate. Moreover, whereas there existed a deputy for the privy seal to take over duties when the keeper was absent, in the signet office there were no signs yet of the forerunner of the modern permanent under-secretary. The four senior

clerks of the signet were all on a footing with each other and entirely
under the personal surveillance of the Secretary, who exercised
supervision over the smallest details of taking orders for parchment,
candles, and red wax as well as more major matters like checking the
actual content of the signet letters. It does not appear to have been an
outstandingly efficient system and was certainly not helped by the
fairly frequent absences of the Secretary himself, who when abroad on
diplomatic business tended to be replaced by an uncommitted member
of another part of the household. Hatteclyffe indeed signed only four
signet letters during his secretaryship. Moreover, as a student* of these
documents has observed: "Some letters are signed by the king alone,
others are countersigned, and others again are signed only by clerks:
some have no signature, and one at least is signed upside down".

In such a fluid situation the play of personality at any one time was
obviously decisive. In the words of the signet clerk George Ashby, in his
poem of 1463 entitled the *Active Policy of a Prince,* a Secretary should
be chosen.

> "with Inspection
> Secrete, sad, and of goode Intencion,
> That can accomplisshe your commaundement
> To thonnour and profit of youre entente".

Commands and their successful accomplishment were indeed the key:
never so entirely as in the Yorkist and early Tudor period did the
Secretary stand or fall by the value of the services he rendered. Already
certain signs of his future role were beginning to manifest themselves.
He was becoming an important negotiating figure, with Hatteclyffe
particularly active in the late 1460s and early 1470s during a protracted
dispute with the Hanse merchants; and signet diplomatic correspondence from Edward IV's reign onwards was no longer confined to the
purpose of paying formal compliments to fellow-princes. About the
same time the Secretary was beginning to engage himself in the
gathering of intelligence. Most portentously of all, the Secretary from
Beckington and after was starting to become a fairly regular member
of the council, though not as yet especially prominent. Nevertheless,
the fact remained that for all this he was never going to become a truly
front-rank figure if he was not allowed to stay in England long enough

*Florence M. G. Higham (née Evans), "A Note on the Pre-Tudor Secretary", in ed.
A. G. Little and F. M. Powicke, *Essays in Medieval History Presented to Thomas
Frederick Tout* (1925), p. 364.

to accomplish properly, and perhaps even influence, the royal commandments. Cometh the hour and the man might not be there.
The early history of the secretaryship is in a sense not unlike astrology: a
study of stars in the ascendancy and fateful conjunctions.

Early Tudor Secretaries: 1495-1534

The period between 1495 and 1534 is perhaps best described as one
of marking time. The Secretaries themselves were interesting and
capable figures, but both Henry VII and Henry VIII stuck (or were
permitted to stick) to traditional household methods of administration.
They failed to realise the potential of the peculiar flexibility embodied
in the person of the Secretary, who with few exceptions continued to be
employed primarily either on diplomatic missions or as a fairly
unthinking factotum dealing with the royal correspondence. A hint of
subsequent responsibilities appeared when Robert Sherborne, the
successor to King, was deputed in the late 1490s to extract dues from
the benighted West-country supporters of Perkin Warbeck, but
this was unusual. Sherborne, soon to be prominent on diplomatic
missions to Rome, was replaced in 1500 by another Oxford man,
Thomas Ruthal, just back from being an envoy in France. Ruthal
was a diligent man, a doctor of canon law, and in 1509 he was
granted the see of Durham. Like King he stayed on as Secretary,
perhaps encouraged by his improving position within the council, on
whose behalf he was beginning to be requested to draw up various
minutes. We catch a glimpse of Ruthal in secretarial action in 1509
when, five days after Henry VII's death and with Fuensalida having
been summoned to attend the council, it was he who, following a
private conference with the new king in another part of the building,
appeared in the doorway to tell the Spanish ambassador that the
marriage with Catherine would still go ahead. In the last years of his
secretaryship, however, Ruthal came increasingly under the domination of Wolsey; and Giustiniani later refers to his "singing treble to the
cardinal's bass". Ruthal also seems to have suffered mortification, even
actual physical illness, when on one occasion, having been requested to
compile a tally of the kingdom's worth, he presented to Henry VIII by
an unfortunate mischance a written account of his own not inconsider-
able possessions. In 1516 he became keeper of the privy seal, no longer

necessarily the promotion it once had been, and was succeeded by
Richard Pace.

Pace, an experienced diplomatist and well-known figure in moderate
reforming humanist circles, in fact assumed the secretaryship while
still engaged on a fruitless mission in Switzerland. There he stayed for
up to a year longer and only managed to subdue his irritation by
composing the treatise *De Fructu*. The book praised the life of poverty,
but Erasmus criticised it as "very feeble" and tartly observed of the
author that "meanwhile he enjoys good fortune, is rich, and is the
favourite of king and cardinal". Nevertheless, there was no denying
Pace's learning, and in October 1518, following the celebration in St
Paul's of the treaty of London, a contemporary referred to "the recital
of a very elegant and grave oration on the peace by the chief
Secretary". As Secretary he proved to be the first of the grumblers,
writing from Windsor in October 1520 of how his royal master "spares
no pains to convert the sport of hunting into a martyrdom". But the
selfless toil could pay off, as when in September 1521 Pace was able to
write to Wolsey, then in Calais, with a smug sense of being in the know:
"It was lately the king's pleasure to dispute with your Grace, and now it
is his pleasure to hold his peace". Indeed, it was this question of
access to the king's ear, the source of authority, which without doubt
lay behind the persistent and scarcely-concealed rivalry between the
Secretary and the jealous cardinal. As early as 1519 Pace had endured
a terrible time when, sent abroad without precise instructions, he had
had to ·wait almost a month before Wolsey consented to post him
details of what exactly his diplomatic mission was. Contemporaries
readily interpreted the struggle in terms of Wolsey doing all he could
to keep Pace as much as possible away from Henry. The tradition
permeated down to Shakespeare, who in *Henry VIII* has Cardinal
Campeius cautioning Wolsey following the dismissal of Pace:

"They will not stick to say you envied him
And, fearing he would rise, he was so virtuous,
Kept him a foreign man still; which so grieved him
That he ran mad and died . . ."

Wolsey's curt response, "We fear not to be grip'd by meaner persons",
pleases dramatically, but is hardly consistent with what we know of the
man.

Tensions were apparent even during Pace's frequent absences, when in effect he was replaced as Secretary by Sir Thomas More, who had been in the royal service since at least 1517. More during these phases treated Wolsey with studied deference and was careful to be the entirely passive middleman in the correspondence between the king and his chancellor that was necessary when they were in different places. In 1526 Pace was formally relieved of his office, if not yet because of his incipient insanity, certainly as an unacceptably melancholic figure for a busy man of affairs. His successor was William Knight, who had served Henry VII in a quasi-secretarial capacity, his son as a diplomatist, and endeared himself to Wolsey as someone who "hath no colour or acquaintance". In August 1512 it had been Knight, getting in training for the burdens of the secretaryship, who had been delegated to go ahead of the abjectly returning party and inform Henry of the complete failure of the Anglo-Spanish attempt on Aquitaine. Now as Secretary his age (he was in his fifties), his fading eyesight, the seemingly impossible situation that was developing over Henry and his divorce, his fraught attempt to wrest concessions from the captive pope — these all combined to give Knight a miserable three years in office. In December 1527 he came within a whisker of being murdered at Monterotundo, a few miles outside Rome. By 1528 he was openly confessing the divorce problem to be intractable. And in July 1529 he was succeeded by Stephen Gardiner, who earlier in the year had also tried his luck at whispering into the frightened but also obstinate papal ear.

Gardiner himself was a formidable lawyer, master of Trinity Hall, Cambridge, and fresh from being Wolsey's private secretary. He wrote to a friend on receiving the signet into his keeping: "I take up my residence at court today. You will, as I hope, shortly see an advance in my fortunes". The same day he wrote to the unhappy Wolsey to explain why he could not see his old master personally: "His Highness, having before my coming appointed me a chamber and spoken for mine allowance, gave me special commandment not to depart hence". And a week later he wrote again to Wolsey: "I have been forth from morn to night a-hunting by the King's Highness' commandment". Now manifestly the king's man, Gardiner as Secretary steadily diversified his activities, was granted as a reward in 1531 the extremely wealthy

see of Winchester, and the next year, away on a short diplomatic
mission in France, had his absence lamented by Henry as akin to "the
lack of my right hand". Ironically though, and also illuminatingly, this
very absence afforded Thomas Cromwell the opportunity to make
significant inroads into the royal confidence. Moreover, on his return
from France, Gardiner led Convocation in its short-lived struggle to
withstand the Supplication against the Ordinaries and by so doing
committed the gravest secretarial sin of openly disobeying the royal
will. The French ambassador Du Bellay had pertinently observed of
Gardiner in October 1529 that he would "have a good deal to do with
the management of affairs, especially if he will abandon his order".
But Gardiner did not shed his ecclesiastical identity and thereby
indirectly hastened the coming of the lay Secretary. By 1533 at the
latest Cromwell was in effect the King's Secretary, by April 1534
formally so. Gardiner retired to Winchester, perhaps not altogether
unhappy to fight his conservative fight another day and from a
non-secretarial vantage point. Doubtless he remembered how in
Marseilles the previous November, in the presence of Pope Clement
and King Francis I of France, the news that Henry was refusing to
retract his position had earned him a bitter rebuke from Francis, who
had just managed to secure a delay in the promulgation of Henry's
excommunication: "As fast as I study to win the pope, ye study to lose
him. Ye, ye have clearly marred all". The attack was entirely unfair,
but the phenomenon of the Secretary taking the rap for royal failings
was subsequently to become all too familiar.

The tomb of Thomas Beckington.

Photograph by S. W. Kenyon, by permission of the Dean and Chapter of Wells Cathedral

Thomas Cromwell. By an unknown artist after Hans Holbein the Younger, c. 1534.
National Portrait Gallery

Sir Thomas Smith. By Paul Fisher after Holbein, c. 1546.
*By permission of Provost and Fellows of Eton
Photograph Courtauld Institute of Art*

Sir William Petre. By Steven van der Muelen, 1567.
Essex Record Office, by permission of Hon. John Petre

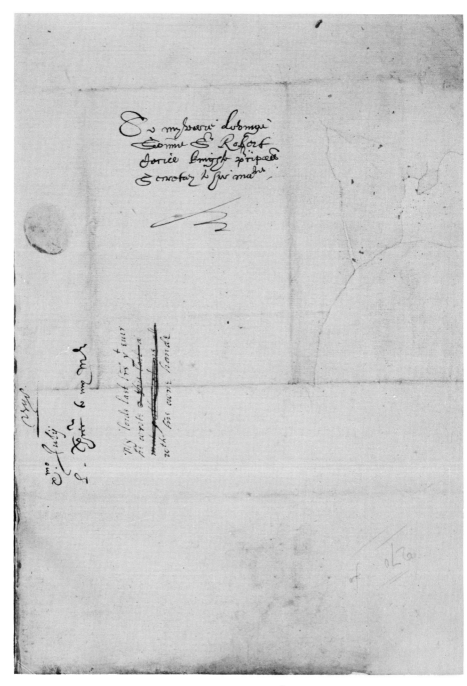

Burghley's last autograph letter. To his son Robert, serving of the Queen, for all other service is indeed b[

Thoughe I know you coūt it yowr duty, in nature so
contynually, to show yow carefull of my state of
helth, yet war I also vnnaturall, if I should not
tak comfort therby, and to besek almighty god
to bless yow w' supply of such blessyng as I cā not
in this infirmyte yeld yow

only I pray yow diligently and effectvally, let hir
May vnderstaad how hir syngular kyndnes doth
overcō my power to aceptt it. who though she will
not be a mother, yet she showeth hir selfe by
fedyng me w' hir own princely hand, as a carefull noris

and if I may be wayned to fede my self, I shall
be more redy to serve hir o' y' erth, if not, I hope
to be in heavē a pentor for hir and gods church.
and so I thank yow for your physiches./

serve god by pryg of y' Quene for
all other price is m derk bondage to
y' devill

10 Feb 1598

Yowr languishyg
fath' W Burghley

Sir William Cecil. Possibly by or after Arnold van Brounckhorst, c. 1560-70.

National Portrait Gallery

Sir Francis Walsingham. Probably by John de Critz the Elder, c. 1585.
National Portrait Gallery

Sir Robert Cecil. By John de Critz the Elder, 1602.

By courtesy of the marquess of Salisbury

CHAPTER TWO

Thomas Cromwell: 1534-40

"A kite flying with royal eagles, a jay chattering in a golden cage".

THIS view of Thomas Cromwell as a distasteful upstart — here expressed by his contemporary George Cavendish, Cardinal Wolsey's gentleman usher — was to persist. In the eighteenth century the local authorities of Leeds, offered a statue of Cromwell, felt forced to decline it on account of the popular resentment they feared it would engender. Moreover, historians until fairly recently have not hesitated to draw facile comparisons between Cromwell and Machiavelli and to treat the Englishman as a not dissimilar symbol of ruthless and entirely secular power-seeking. Certainly he was a formidable character with an extremely sharp tongue. After Lord Dacre on one occasion had been acquitted by his peers of a charge of treason, with Cromwell absent because of an attack of gout, he is reputed to have gone through the routine of thanking the Secretary for his help in bringing about the verdict, to which Cromwell merely growled back "Thank my legs!" In a wider sense, however, recent work by G. R. Elton above all has entirely redressed the picture. It is now clear that Cromwell, while undoubtedly a master politician, was also a humane intellectual, a Protestant by conviction, and a generous if often thwarted social reformer. He also instigated changes in government with a zeal which can only be described as revolutionary. The Elizabethan writer Gabriel Harvey gives one an idea of the essence of the man's ability

19

when he compared him thus to the church-based intelligentsia of the time: "The Lord Cromwell, by the only promptness of his wit, facility of speech, and a pragmatical dexterity to all purposes, overshadowed and obscured even our greatest clerks". Indeed, the need now in terms of appreciating Cromwell is less to open one's eyes than not to be bewildered by his omnicompetent virtuosity into overestimating the extent of his permanent achievement.

Cromwell's personal background was rugged. He was born about 1485, emerged out of a small-time entrepreneurial Putney family, earned his living at various times as a soldier, a merchant, and a solicitor, and made his mark politically in the 1520s under the auspices of Wolsey, managing at the end of the decade to get off the legatine shipwreck just in time. By 1530 he was in the royal service. This is not the place to discuss the question of who ultimately lay behind the break with Rome — "king or minister?" — but it is worth mentioning certain facets of Henry's temperament that remained significant through the 1530s. He was a vain man, cruel, and liable to sudden impulsive shifts. The image and the sense of power were what counted in his monarchical opinion, not the tedious day-to-day deskwork on which governmental authority was in reality becoming increasingly grounded. Put another way, though he made the decisions, he only did so when he realised there was a decision to be made. Obviously the Henrician Reformation was not something to be done behind Henry's back; but nor on the other hand does its inner coherence sit at all easily on the king's volatile frame. At the very least Cromwell's role must have been an extremely important one. To chart the precise chronology of Cromwell's rise to power is almost impossible, and of course begs the key questions, but as early as August 1532 Gardiner in France was sending him a commission to be sent out under the signet and adding the plea that "to the doing whereof you must necessarily help or it shall I fear me be undone". Anyway, in April 1534 Cromwell formally became Principal Secretary (as the office was becoming increasingly called, partly as a reflection of its relative rise in status, partly to differentiate it from the rapidly fading secretaries of the Latin and French tongues), and from that date we must focus our attention.

One of the problems is the overlapping of Cromwell's secular offices. In April 1533 he had become chancellor of the exchequer, in October

1534 he was to become master of the rolls, and in July 1536 lord privy seal. Yet it is difficult not to feel that for most of the time, from 1534 to 1540, the secretaryship was the functional mainspring of his work. Over quite a long period it had been gradually growing in importance; it permitted continuous access to the royal confidence if used in the right way; it had potentially at least an unrivalled flexibility; and while entirely responsive to the individual holder, it yet allowed plenty of scope for bureaucratic development to raise it to the status of one of the great offices. Cromwell was a new man, as he was not often allowed to forget, and the office must have felt just right for someone of his wonderfully plastic cast of mind.

Cromwell as Secretary

It was to be expected that Cromwell as Secretary would want to give the signet more formal authority relative to the other seals, especially after Gardiner had become the first Secretary to put his signature to signet warrants as a matter of habit. The act of 1536 "concerning the Clerks of the Signet and Privy Seals" may or may not have been of Cromwell's instigation, but certainly he was not opposed to it. The main points of the measures were fourfold: it insisted that either the Secretary or a signet clerk scrutinise any item that was eventually to be issued under the great seal; it further insisted that the clerks of the signet and the privy seal receive their fees even when the monarch issued an immediate warrant; it determined what these fees were to be; and it reiterated the principles of the council ordinance of 1444. As a piece of legislation it was deceptively simple, apparently seeking to assign to the signet the pivotal role in the everyday working of government which the privy seal had enjoyed for much of the previous two centuries. But in practice the age of government by seals was virtually over and a more familiar, literate style of getting things done was taking its place. Instead, the measures of 1536 demand a rather more low-profile interpretation: Cromwell was merely seeking to tidy up the business of the seals and in so doing ensure parity at least for the signet; while by emphasising the question of fees Cromwell hoped to promote a more assiduous, less favour-currying clerkship. If the legislation did amount to significantly more than that, one senses that behind it lay the person of the Secretary himself and his overriding desire to create more room within which to operate. As Elton points out so pertinently about the act, it regarded both the signet and the privy seal "simply as instruments which had to be affixed to documents giving effect to decisions taken elsewhere and to be transmitted elsewhere again". Moreover, when Cromwell did use the signet in a more positive role between 1536 and 1540, he did so less by issuing warrants under it that would eventually reach chancery via the privy seal (this pedantic, old-fashioned approach he left to the Secretaries who came after him that felt the need to employ it), but rather by issuing under the signet a whole range of letters of question and instruction to men of influence in the localities. The personal touch was all-important; and it dominated Cromwell's attitude towards the signet office in his charge as well as the signet itself.

Again, the formal appearance of Cromwell's actions was misleading. The act of July 1534 concerning the organisation of the signet office suggests him applying much-needed reform in a straightforward, commonsensical enough manner. So he was: the measures insist on a strict division of labour as well as rewards, regulate the methods by which this was to be achieved, and throughout approach the hitherto ramshackle signet office in terms of promoting a greater sense of corporate responsibility. In the event, however, the six years of Cromwell's secretaryship were years of overlap and confusion between the work of his own emerging private secretariat and the duties and allegiances of the actual signet office. Thomas Wriothesley was a prime case in point. He became a clerk of the signet in 1530 and by about 1537 was virtually the chief clerk. Yet he had been in Cromwell's employ since 1524; and from 1534 he in effect assumed the job of being the Principal Secretary's private secretary. It was in that capacity, thoroughly personal, that Wriothesley exercised his pre-dominant influence over the other clerks. The case of Ralph Sadler was somewhat different, but equally revealing. Though likewise growing up as a young man in Cromwell's household, he tended to be employed by Cromwell from about 1535 increasingly in the capacity of staying close to the king, keeping a tight rein on the Norfolk and Gardiner faction, and adding a persistent voice in favour of Crom-wellian proposals. His role was reflected in the note he sent to Cromwell on 11th January 1536 about the problem of getting Henry to authorise bills: "I shall do the best I can albeit as you know his grace is always loathe to sign". Inwards to keep a watch on the king, outwards to ensure the implementation of decisions, Cromwell had in Sadler and Wriothesley respectively his two main agents in smoothing the increasingly complex secretarial path. It was an efficient system, extremely so, yet at root, one must emphasise, it was personal and not "bureaucratic", in the modern sense of the term. Long before Cromwell, ministers as well as kings had nurtured civil servants; and it was to be a long time after Cromwell before civil servants began in any consistent way to stick to their department during a time of change rather than to their particular master, be he king or minister. Cromwell's greatness as Secretary lay instead in his unique abilities as a functioning being. Without precedent, and almost solely by virtue of what he actually *did* in the day-to-day sense, he transformed the position of King's Secretary into an office of state — and this at a time, moreover, when almost all the other old household positions were losing ground. To see how he did it one must study him, and no other, in secretarial action.

Perhaps Cromwell's most felicitous device was the way in which he gained virtual control over the privy council. Wolsey in the 1520s had attempted to reform the old council, but it was Cromwell as Secretary who gave the institution cohesion, intimacy, and a sense of purpose. The ace up his sleeve was the fact that, as Secretary and therefore the member of the council with the least social status, he it was who tended to be called on to speak first and thus as it frequently turned out was put in a position where he could dominate the proceedings. Cromwell used the inverted privilege immaculately: he would draw up the agenda before the council met and then, during the actual meeting, take the council through it at his own pace. He more than anyone knew the facts of each situation and this gave him an inestimable advantage. In addition, it was Cromwell who was generally turned to in order to execute the council's decisions or at least to inform the authorities concerned of what needed to be done. An indication of the Secretary's indispensability came in 1539 when the earl of Southampton, about to go off to Calais on official business, arrived at court to get his orders from the council and expressed the hope that Cromwell would not be absent, lest otherwise he be delayed in his departure.

Nevertheless, during and for quite a long while after Cromwell's time, a wise Secretary never forgot that it was essentially as the royal instrument within the privy council that he acted, however much his ordering of business and attention to detail helped (especially during the Elizabethan epoch) to enhance the governmental authority and policy-making status of the actual council. The era of cabinet ministers responsible to Parliament was certainly not yet.

Cromwell as Secretary spent much of his time attempting to enforce throughout the country obedience to the Henrician Reformation; and in so doing he brought the massively diverse, unrelenting question of internal security for the first time proper into the secretarial province. His methods were appropriately ramified — including the commissioning of propagandist tracts, oath-taking for office-holders, and (probably against his own will) a harshly inflexible proclamation of 1538 attempting to prevent the reading of subversive books. One of Cromwell's favourite ploys was the circular letter, forerunner of the usual form of communication adopted by the Elizabethan privy council. He began the habit of sending out these letters in April 1535 and used them to urge upon men of local influence the need both to be vigilant and to bring before the Secretary any apparently deviant spirits. Typical was a circular of June 1535: Cromwell, doubtful of how thoroughly the episcopacy had made the break with Rome, instructed sheriffs and justices to undertake "diligent search, wait and espial in any place in your sheriffwick whether the said bishop do truly, sincerely, and without all manner cloak, colour or dissimulation, execute and accomplish our will and commandment". Even more central to Cromwell's methods was his voluminous correspondence with particular individuals. On 13th July 1534, for example, he wrote in generous appreciation to the earl of Shrewsbury: "I thank evermore your Lordship for your good zeal, diligence, and dexterity in repressing and apprehending such pernicious and detestable felons: and thereof shall I not fail to make true report to his Highness who I am assured shall take the same in most thankful part". Cromwell's dependence on the goodwill of noblemen like Shrewsbury, and gentry almost everywhere, was absolute: the state could never have afforded a centralised police system, even if it had been considered desirable. But the alternative system of informal correspondence could not have worked either without the ceaseless personal involvement of the Secretary himself.

Cromwell's record as a cross-examiner of suspects is evidence enough: during the 1530s he questioned with scrupulous care some 350 people accused of speaking treason, of whom only 40 received the death penalty as a result. Casting a wide net but throwing back most of the catch, Cromwell made the government something to be feared by those in the apparently remote localities who would disturb the new order, but something to trust for those who would place an informer's confidence in it. Henry was sufficiently sensible to be apprehensive of overburdening Cromwell, writing to Southampton in September 1539 that "I would for no good that his mind should be so troubled that it should cast him into any disease". Yet precisely in the Secretary's ubiquitous ability to deal with all manner of tasks lay his effective power. He kept not only the country at large tractable, but also Parliament. This could involve thoughtful strategy in addition to the usual attempts to manipulate elections. In 1536, for example, amidst growing reactionary mutterings of discontent, Cromwell shrewdly advised Henry "to grant few licences for any to be absent from the Parliament", a gambit designed to ensure a full turn-out on the part of the king's supporters at least. Indeed, in terms of secretarial history, the only major sphere in which Cromwell did not shine and thereby leave a precedent for his successors was that of diplomacy and its attendant practices of intelligence-gathering from abroad. Moreover, when he did try his hand at the art, a certain lack of expertise contributed materially to his own downfall.

Cromwell's Fall

Cromwell's unpopularity in certain quarters, inevitable during a decade of such change, had particularly manifested itself during the Pilgrimage of Grace in 1536, when the rebels' songs had berated him as a low-born shearman who gave evil counsel to the king. But the Pilgrimage had been a local rising, which could be treated as a matter of subverted loyalties rather than alternative policies. By about 1539, however, Cromwell was coming under a more specific political threat from the conservative and Catholic grouping led by Norfolk and Gardiner. Almost certainly, moreover, he was beginning to doubt

Henry's continuing attachment to him. An odd but perhaps truthful private letter of 1538 written by George Paulet, brother of the better-known William, depicts Cromwell grinning and bearing it as any good Secretary had to: "The king beknaveth him twice a week and sometimes knocks him well about the pate; and yet when that he hath been well pummelled about the head and shaken up as it were a dog, he will come out of the Great Chamber shaking off the bush with as merry a countenance as though he might rule all the roost". The bone of contention in 1539 between Cromwell and the Catholics were the backward-looking Six Articles. Henry allowed them to be passed, but Cromwell showed that he was still managing to hold his own in the factional struggle by persuading the king that the actual implementation of the articles should be delayed. Meanwhile, the question of the proposed royal marriage to Anne of Cleves was becoming of increasingly critical concern. The initiative came from Henry himself — "I trust on no one but myself" he had observed in 1538 about this matter of finding a new wife — but Cromwell's error was in allowing himself to be identified too closely with the candidature of Anne and its manifest Protestant connotations. And when Henry first met the disappointing Anne in January 1540 it was all that Cromwell could do to stop the king making a run for it. Cromwell was not in fact to fall directly because of Anne; but Henry's personal confidence in him, ever dependent on latitude to fulfil inclinations rather than duties, was now badly shaken.

Three months later, in April 1540, not long after Henry had banished Anne from court, Sadler and Wriothesley became Principal Secretaries in place of Cromwell, who himself became earl of Essex and great chamberlain of England. Clearly he remained a force to be reckoned with. Indeed, in the light of the personal backgrounds of Sadler and Wriothesley, it is difficult not to view the change in the secretaryship in Cromwellian as much as Henrician terms. Cromwell, who had only recently secured the election of the two aides to Parliament, doubtless hoped that the new boost to their status would enable them to represent himself as well as the king more effectively in the Commons, a need which had become increasingly pressing since Cromwell's own elevation to the peerage, as Lord Cromwell of Wimbledon, in 1536. There were other reasons as well. Cromwell also probably hoped that Sadler and Wriothesley would as Secretaries be even better placed to continue their respective tasks of staying close to the king and supervising the control of political patronage which he had built up as sole Secretary. He must also have hoped for added support on the council. But perhaps above all, Cromwell may have dreamt of a freer role, influencing and creating policy on a grand scale quite impossible in the context of the weight of pettiness imposed by the everyday secretarial work burden. If so, and it was a legitimate enough dream considering the strides Cromwell had taken during the 1530s and the scope of his aspirations, he was to be rudely disenchanted.

For a few more weeks after April 1540 he continued to use Wriothesley as his private secretary, without realising the extent to which even a long-standing servant must inevitably become the king's man once he was formally appointed Secretary. The irony was considerable: Cromwell more than anyone had made the secretaryship into what it had become, a central instrument of royal authority, but now, with Catherine Howard rising fast and the Norfolk faction working hard on the fickle king with heresy scare stories, he paid the price. Sadler is reputed to have shown a certain degree of personal loyalty following Cromwell's arrest in June 1540, but he hardly seems to have committed himself during the crucial days leading up to the arrest. Wriothesley was a plain turncoat who a few years later received the lord chancellorship as his reward. On 28th July Cromwell was executed. Within a year his king, in a mood of persistent ill-humour, was regretting the deed and blaming the presence of misleading influences around him. He knew he had thrown away a minister of extraordinary ability. And some thirty years later, in a pamphlet entitled *Discourse on Usury,* one of Cromwell's successors as Principal Secretary, the learned Thomas Wilson, was moved to exclaim: "And shall I name one who hath been in our age, and wish him now to live to cure so great a canker? Would God England had a Cromwell: I will say no more". Certainly they are tempting last words on the man.

The Extent of the Cromwellian Achievement

In January 1526 the household ordinances drawn up at Eltham put the Secretary on a footing with the vice-chamberlain of the household in terms of the number of horses (eight) and beds for servants (three) allowed to him while he was resident at court. It was hardly a magnificent allocation and was symptomatic of the Secretary's still relatively lowly social status. Doubtless also it was one of the reasons why Cromwell assumed the additional office of the lord privy seal in 1536. By 1539, however, the social position of the Secretary had become somewhere near commensurate with the recently-developed extent of his responsibilities. In terms of precedence in the House of Lords he was now ranked above barons and bishops without office and was considered junior only to the great established officers of state. A certain decline in standing followed the succession of Sadler and Wriothesley to the secretaryship in 1540, but this was only temporary and did not affect the fact that during Cromwell's period of office the functional base had been laid for the long-term rise in secretarial status over the next two centuries. Yet the central paradox remained: although because of Cromwell the secretaryship assumed in role a public significance which it had never had before, nevertheless each holder of the office remained for a very long time, at least up to William III's reign, as dependent as ever on royal support. And during that time Secretaries continued to be important figures because of, rather than in spite of, the existence of strong monarchs sensible enough to perceive the potential of these new officers of state as a means of controlling oppositional movements. The problem was, of course, that not all monarchs were sensible enough, even if they did have pretensions to strength.

CHAPTER THREE

PRINCIPAL SECRETARIES: 1540-1612

1540 (March): Sir Thomas Wriothesley
1544 (March): Sir William Petre

1540 (March): Sir Ralph Sadler
1543 (23rd April): Sir William Paget (leaving the office June 1547)
1548 (17th April): Sir Thomas Smith
1549 (15th October): Dr. Nicholas Wotton
1550 (5th September): William Cecil
1553 (2nd June): Sir John Cheke (additional)
1553 (August): Sir John Bourne (until March 1558)

1557 (30th March): Sir John Boxall
1558 (20th November): Sir William Cecil
1572 (13th July): Sir Thomas Smith (died August 1577)

1573 (21st December): Sir Francis Walsingham (died April 1590)

1577 (12th November): Thomas Wilson (died June 1581)
1586 (30th September): William Davison (dismissed 1587)
1596 (5th July): Sir Robert Cecil (died May 1612)

1600 (10th May): John Herbert (appointed "second Secretary of State") (died July 1619)

The Age of the Cecils: 1540-1612
I. narrative

"Councillors of State must deal like wise physicians, that do apply the remedy agreeable to the nature of the patient, and not that which may seem most proper for the disease".

THIS grievance expressed by Sir Francis Walsingham in 1585 was thoroughly typical of the feelings of most Secretaries both before and after him towards their monarchs. The friction was inherent in the position. Almost half a century earlier, in the sign-manual warrant of 1540 appointing Sadler and Wriothesley as Henry's Principal Secretaries, even the document's formal and convoluted language could not disguise the essentially royal capacity of the new appointees. "Good service" on behalf of his Majesty was the theme, however Cromwellian in a political sense their elevation may have been. The warrant of 1540 had other points of interest also. A complicated section explained how the two Secretaries, both now knights, would alternate in attendance between the Lords and the Commons, although in practice this came to little, since almost invariably Secretaries continued to be far more valuable building up a body of royal followers in the lower house. More important was the warrant's stress on the equality of the two Secretaries, symbolised by the fact that they were each to be in possession of not just a signet seal, but also "a book containing all such things as shall pass by either of their hands". Each

Secretary, the warrant went on, was "to be made ever privy to the other's register". And the warrant concluded with the unequivocal resolution that Sadler and Wriothesley were to "have, enjoy, and use the place of the Principal Secretary as heretofore have been accustomed". Cromwell's legacy was clear: now it was up to the Secretaries to make of it what they could.

Henry VIII's Last Secretaries: 1540-47

Lloyd's *Statesmen and Worthies* of the mid-seventeenth century refers thus to Sadler: "King Henry understood two things: 1. A Man: 2. A Dish of Meat; and was seldom deceived in either: for a Man, none more compleat than Sir Ralph, who was at once an exquisite writer and a most valiant and experienced soldier". Sadler was also a capable politician who never made the mistake of aiming too high. What by temperament he was not, however, was a creative statesman. "I can not endure the spending of that time in designing an action which might perform two", he once actually admitted, in so doing revealing why he never rose above being a second-ranker. When in January 1541 he was arrested and tried, as a Cromwellian, he was soon acquitted precisely because his head was reckoned of far less value than his writing arm. Sadler spent most of the rest of the year in a slough, staying in London with the unconsidered part of the council while his fellow-Secretary attended the king and the influential section of the council elsewhere. By the end of 1541, however, following the revelations concerning Catherine Howard, Sadler was back in the royal presence and on 7th December confidently instructing the council "to pick out from the testimony given" in order to clinch the conviction against the Howards and their associates. In the event it was not to be such a clean sweep: during 1542 a compromise emerged between the groupings; and Sadler, helped by his personal anti-French animus, was careful to adopt a friendly attitude towards Chapuys in the course of the negotiations that preceded the Spanish treaty of 1543. He had learnt from the fate of his old master and was prepared to stomach his Protestant qualms. Indeed, it was a mark of his usefulness, though a source of chagrin to Sadler himself, when in March 1543 he was sent to Edinburgh to represent the English interest and a few weeks later was replaced as Secretary by William Paget. As a gesture of recompense Sadler received the office of master of the great wardrobe.

Wriothesley, the other new Secretary of 1540, is a difficult figure to pin down. Cromwell was not alone in discovering that the man's political morality was as slippery as his name suggested. As the balance swung during 1541 Wriothesley deserted the ostentatiously Catholic camp which he had so recently joined and, with no apparent difficulty, took a leading part in going systematically through all the potentially damaging reports relating to the queen. The council was then able to go ahead and (as he told the perhaps rather impression-able Sadler on 4th December) "pick out what served their business". Indeed, according to his cousin, the chronicler Charles Wriothesley, it had been he who on 13th November had gone "to Hampton Court to the Queen, and called all the ladies and gentlewomen and her servants into the Great Chamber, and there openly afore them declared certain offences that she had done in misusing her body with certain persons afore the King's time, wherefore he there discharged all her household". From 1542, however, Wriothesley played the Imperial card for all it was worth and was influential in the eventual Anglo-Spanish agreement to co-operate in invading France in 1544. Like Sadler he seems to have perceived early on what was to become a key secretarial precept, namely that secular nationalist considerations must increasingly transcend religious factional differences. In January 1544 he was created Baron Wriothesley of Titchfield; and three months later he succeeded Audley as lord chancellor.

Wriothesley's successor was Sir William Petre, who over the next thirteen years was to keep one end going while his colleagues came and went. He had learnt his trade under Cromwell and had been a particularly effective agent in the dissolution of the monasteries. Luckily for his career he just managed in 1539 to wriggle out of the task of being sent to Cleves to inspect the royal daughters there. Petre was ideal secretarial material: silent and watchful, though perhaps almost excessively cautious. Contemporaries viewed him with little compunction as essentially a conscientious hack. On one occasion, indeed, Chapuys was only comforted in his own mind that there could be nothing as major in the air as an Anglo-French alliance when he heard that it was Petre, and not Paget, who was going on the particular embassy to France. Yet it is easy to underestimate him. Certainly his splashing out of £9 on a new coat and gown after he had been appointed Secretary was the gesture of a born civil servant surprisingly promoted; while soon afterwards, during the preparations for the French expedition, it was apparent for all to see that the new Secretary's offering of barely a handful of footmen was the least of any councillor's. Nevertheless, by the very fact of his assiduous attention to detail, Petre before long began to establish for himself a secure foothold in the royal administration. In the absence of Henry, and of Paget also for much of the time, Petre spent a difficult summer in 1544 trying by circular letters to raise money for the army; but once Henry was back in England, Petre's self-assurance increased and he began to issue firm directives to the part of the council that remained in Boulogne. By November he was even bold enough to command the arrogant Sir Thomas Seymour, Admiral of the Fleet, to "have henceforth a more wary eye to your victuals, considering with what difficulty and charge they are brought to you". Paget recognised his colleague's new strength and began to permit him to inspect at draft stage some of his own letters to the council, as he had been doing from the first to those drawn up by Petre. This is not to deny that Petre remained throughout the pedantic bureaucrat rather than the ambitious minister. He did — but in his devotion to the unconsidered trifles of administration he helped lay the secretarial groundwork that in future even the most ambitious of his successors would only abandon at peril.

As for Paget, knighted after a year as Secretary, he was a self-made Londoner who became a professional royal servant at his best dealing with patronage and foreign affairs. Suitably, it was from an arduous embassy in Paris that he was recalled in April 1543 to take over from Sadler. It proved a deceptive release: Paget as Secretary was to go abroad on five diplomatic missions, of which the most fraught was the one at Boulogne in the early summer of 1546. The French were erratic in their negotiations, while Henry from the other side of the channel insisted on a stringent cartographical check of the proposed terms; and Paget, in fact only a few days before the peace was settled, stressed in a letter to Henry that the delay had certainly not been caused by an absence of "stoutness" on his own part. The Secretary was no stranger to this type of chequered diplomacy, for in March 1545, while conducting negotiations at Brussels with Imperial representatives, he had equally noted in a letter in cipher to Petre that "dissimulation, vanity, flattery, and unshamefastness reign most here, and with the same they be rencountered". Paget's own political career advanced smoothly. He used his secretarial position to infiltrate his way increasingly into the ageing king's confidence; he dispensed such presents to the young Prince Edward as a sandbox; and after Henry's death he was in a position to reveal what the former king's wishes had been about the allocation of patronage in the new reign. "The said King devised with me apart, as it is well known he used to open his pleasure to me alone in many things", he boasted at the time, and was apparently believed. During a minority, however, the position of Secretary was inevitably for a while devalued. Paget perceived this and in June 1547 abandoned the office to become formally comptroller of the king's household and also sole chancellor of the Duchy of Lancaster, but informally Protector Somerset's most valued confidant. It had been a remarkable rise. Referring to the Secretary's father, a sergeant-at-mace, the youthful earl of Surrey, on trial for his life in January 1547, had addressed Paget with these haughty but unavailing words: "Thou, Catchpole, thou hadst better hold thy tongue, for the kingdom has never been well since the King put mean creatures like thee in the government". Within days Henry was dead and in the absence of a dominating monarch the importance of the Secretaries, these pernicious "new men", diminished accordingly.

Edwardian and Marian Secretaries: 1547-58

No one replaced Paget as Secretary until Sir Thomas Smith was appointed in April 1548. With John Cheke and William Cecil he had formed at Cambridge in the early 1540s a circle of Greek scholars inclined towards humanism and public matters. Smith himself came from a typically "secretarial" family background: small-scale sheep-farming in Essex. But his intellectual was always greater than his political prowess, for he seems to have lacked both human perception and what his biographer describes as "nervous stamina". He emerged as Secretary under Somerset's star and waned with his master too. For a year at least this attachment allowed Smith the degree of political prominence necessary to satisfy his personal vanity. During the summer of 1548 he vigorously pursued boycott tactics to win back the privileges of the English merchants based at Antwerp; while in December, attending a meeting of the bishops to discuss the forthcoming Prayer Book, Smith forcefully attacked those present with Catholic inclinations. Smith himself was of an unashamedly secular outlook and possessed of a tongue that during the course of his secretaryship was increasingly resented by both religious wings. In June 1549, moreover, Smith lost his most important friend when, in the context of rapidly mounting social and economic troubles, he vainly cautioned Somerset against the long-term dangers of debasing the coinage. Soon afterwards he went into a period of rustication at Eton, during which gloomy time he probably wrote the renowned treatise entitled *A Discourse of the Commonweal of England*. He returned to politics in the autumn, only to find himself a victim of the fall of Somerset. At the crucial stage luck went against him: whereas Petre was fortunate enough to be sent by Somerset from Hampton Court to London in order to talk terms with Northumberland and his party on the council there, from where he decided wisely not to return, Smith found himself early in October stranded impotently at Windsor Castle with the equally powerless King Edward. Petre, after being frantically petitioned by his colleague, was considerate enough in this crisis to send Smith's brother to the castle with up-to-date news of the situation in London. But it proved meagre consolation: Smith was soon hauled before the council and forced to abase himself. Even after this he was imprisoned on 13th October and two days later replaced as Secretary by Nicholas Wotton. Like a true scholar the prisoner in the Tower turned for comfort to the study of astrology and the composition of bad verse.

Wotton was by temperament and training a skilful diplomatist who now endured an uneasy eleven months as Secretary. He was also dean of Canterbury and York; and Lloyd later wrote of him: "This was that rare man that was made for all business — so dexterous! This was he that was made for all times — so complying! This was he who lived Doctor of both laws, and died Doctor of both Gospels". Wotton was replaced as Secretary in September 1550 by William Cecil. Cecil (who was to be knighted in 1551) had in fact informally acted as Secretary in place of Smith during the late summer of 1549; and with Smith, as

part of the grouping attached to Somerset, he had spent a few wintry
months in the Tower, before both were released simultaneously early
in 1550. Cecil's own background was "new": his father had been a
long-standing minor courtier to Henry VIII, and behind him lay
Welsh yeoman stock. Now as Secretary, he began to sketch in some of
the sincere yet supremely guileful techniques of statecraft that he was
to amplify and almost turn into a mythology of political practice
during his much longer tenure of the office under Queen Elizabeth. As
his keenly Protestant friend Catherine of Suffolk wrote to him, perhaps
cryptically, soon after this first major appointment: "I have ever
thought your wares to be good and saleable".

Cecil proved a duly conscientious Secretary. His colleague Petre
tended to stay close to the king and also concern himself with
diplomatic matters, which left Cecil (as the more convinced, though
never fanatical, Protestant) to run the wishes of Northumberland and
also attend council meetings in London, averaging about four a week.
In November 1550 he began a personal tradition of composing gloomy
memoranda for private circulation with a prognostication characteristically entitled "Indications of imminent danger unless by foresight
diverted". In it he doubted, as he was so often to do, the loyalty of the
population to the Crown rather than the Papacy and stressed the need
for national vigilance. A typical secretarial task, deftly handled, came
Cecil's way in October 1551 when the increasingly isolated Somerset,
only three months away from the scaffold, told the Secretary of his
fears and doubtless hoped for reassuring words. According to King
Edward's journal, "Mr. Cecil answered that if he were not guilty he
might be of good courage, if he were, he had nothing to say but to
lament him". Soon, however, Cecil was beginning to think of such
stoicism in terms of himself. By April 1553, with Edward in his last
illness and Northumberland scheming to alter the royal will, Cecil was
little to be seen either at court or council. But on 2nd June,
Northumberland, in a gesture which clearly indicated that those who
were not with him were against him, appointed as third Secretary (a
precedent in itself) Sir John Cheke, ironically enough Cecil's brother-
in-law through his first marriage as well as his old Cambridge tutor.
Cecil took the point and returned to the centre of affairs. In the end
the outcome was mildly squalid, but perhaps inevitable. On 21st June

the three Secretaries were among the hundred or more leading figures who put their signatures to the settlement of the Crown on Lady Jane Grey, though Cecil did add a futile escape clause that he was only signing "as a witness". Lady Jane Grey's reign in July lasted the proverbial nine days and Cecil steadily if furtively moved towards the anti-Northumberland faction of the council that was demanding the rightful accession of the Catholic Princess Mary. This duly took place, whereupon Cheke and Cecil resigned their offices. Cheke went into exile, but Cecil preferred to play out the reign from the Old Rectory at Wimbledon, though performing the occasional diplomatic mission abroad to demonstrate his continuing supra-religious patriotism. Friends chided him as a time-server, but Cecil's opportunity to serve once again the Protestant cause where it counted was not to be long in coming.

Meanwhile, one must not forget Petre, who had been soldiering on during the Protectorate. During this period he was very much the senior Secretary and seems to have come into his own. He was never particularly close to Somerset and, with the help of his allotted role as a delegate from Hampton Court, survived the scare of October 1549 without too much difficulty. At the last moment though, on the 7th, just before Northumberland and his fellow-conspirators in London sent off Southampton (formerly Wriothesley) to the king with their take-over letter, Petre did make sure that a note was added with the words "almost all your Council being here, we have for the better service of his Majesty caused your Secretary to remain here with us". There was little doubt that in secretarial terms Petre was worth keeping on. In the spring of 1550, following the Anglo-French negotiations in which England agreed to cede Boulogne in return for 400,000 crowns, the French commissioner remarked of him: "Ah, we had gained the other 200,000 crowns, but for the man who said nothing". It was an authentic professional triumph in grim circumstances, but in the last years of the Protectorate the secretarial authority of Petre was severely challenged. The battleground was the boy king: Petre engaged the precocious Edward in plans to make the council's procedure more efficient, but Northumberland more importantly persuaded the king that counter-signatures need not invariably be attached to royal authorisations. It was doubtless a relief to Petre at least when the turbulent reign and its brief aftermath came to an end.

Mary's five years, however, marked a less than glorious phase in secretarial history: the queen's trust and hopes lay elsewhere. Sir John Bourne was appointed Secretary in August 1553 and lasted until March 1558. Little is known about him except that he probably took a firmer stand against the burning of heretics than his colleague, whose accommodating course as Secretary had become almost synonymous with the art of self-survival. Petre indeed was the subject of a notable tribute when Paget wrote late in 1554 to the Emperor Charles: "If Secretary Petre wishes to retire, he ought not to be allowed to do so, but kept in office, for he has been there so long that he is as good as a Council register and reminds the members of everything that has occurred in the past". In fact, though, these were years quite as difficult for Petre as those of the Protectorate. He often had to represent Mary in a hostile Commons; he disliked from the start (however ineffectually) the queen's extremist religious policy; and he was resentful of Philip's attempts to get England to support Spain in a European war. Finally in March 1557 he resigned, though in practice continuing as a loyal work-horse to draft the bulk of the queen's and the council's correspondence and in particular letters of a diplomatic nature. Petre's nominal successor was Sir John Boxall, of whom almost as little is recorded as of Bourne. On Mary's death, however, he seems to have done all he could to clear the way for his successor and provide him with all the relevant information. If so, it was a fitting graciousness, for with the coming in November 1558 of Queen Elizabeth and her loyal councillor William Cecil the secretaryship began to fulfil in a more total sense than hitherto its earlier Cromwellian promise.

William Cecil: 1558-72

Cecil had for some eight years acted in a private capacity as Elizabeth's real estate agent. Now, on 20th November 1558, three days after Mary's death, she appointed him Principal Secretary, charging him that "without respect of my private will you will give me that counsel which you think best; and if you shall know anything necessary to be declared to me of secrecy you shall show it to myself only". For her part, she added, "I will not fail to keep taciturnity therein". The tone reflected the intimate nature of the relationship that was to develop between herself and her Secretary, though in practice Elizabeth was often less than tolerant of hearing public-spirited advice at variance with her personal inclinations. Moreover, only rarely were Elizabeth's ministers permitted the luxury of feeling a sense of permanence about the queen's continuing benevolence towards them. As Robert Naunton (himself a Secretary of State) put it the next century, "all those to whom she distributed her favours were never more than tenants at will". The result tended to be factional in-fighting within the privy council and a ceaseless struggle to attain the royal confidence. Cecil, strategically well-placed as Secretary, was little inclined to allow his Protestant beliefs, "hotter" than those of his royal mistress, to spoil his chances. Catherine of Suffolk, back from Marian exile, wrote to him in 1559 in disgruntled response to that year's compromise religious settlement: "I am forced to say with the prophet Eli, 'How long halt ye between two opinions?'" But in a sense the criticism was unfair, for Catherine would have found the settlement distinctly more anaemic as far as she was concerned if Cecil had not been present to express the voice of responsible Protestantism. And in general Cecil tempered for the rest of his career a pragmatic distaste for Protestant extremists with a firm belief in England's continuing identification with the Protestant cause.

Early in the summer of 1560 Cecil went to Scotland to arrange matters there and Petre deputised for him on an informal basis. The veteran royal servant was now physically in decline and on 19th July, with the queen intending to go on a progress to Portsmouth at the end of the month, he wrote somewhat poignantly to Cecil: "I do much wish that you might be here before her Majesty's remove, for that I am utterly unable to follow unless I should go in a litter, and yet not able to do so without some danger and pain". Cecil too had his problems. Despite having accomplished the treaty of Edinburgh, he was strongly criticised by the queen on his return and was not even allowed travelling expenses. He also found Elizabeth to be increasingly close to Robert Dudley and began privately to talk of resignation. De Quadra, the Spanish ambassador, reported a conversation with Cecil in September in which the Secretary had delivered a gloomy adage to the effect that "it was a bad sailor who did not make for port when he saw a storm coming". But Cecil was not one to give in so easily. In April

1561, after a winter doubtless spent mulling over the problem, he suddenly revealed the existence of a Catholic conspiracy, in which, Cecil guardedly implied, the young Dudley was indirectly involved as a figure-head. The chief object of Cecil's "fears" was the coming Papal nuncio Martinengo, to whom early in May, following intense persuasion by the Secretary, the privy council refused admission. Cecil virtually admitted that the episode was a frame-up when he wrote to a friend on 8th May about the conspiring pawns in his game: "I mean no evil to any of them, but only for the rebating of the papists' humours which by the Queen's Majesty's lenity grew too rank". The ploy served Cecil's purposes well enough. Indeed, he had already in December 1560 affirmed his long-term ambitions by becoming master of the court of wards but at the same time keeping on the secretaryship. "Whereby", a contemporary noted, "he declares his ability for the execution of many offices without other aid".

The succession issue dominated Cecil's thoughts during the 1560s. He wrote to Throckmorton, ambassador in France in July 1561: "God send our Mistress a husband, and by time a son, that we may hope our posterity shall have a masculine succession. This matter is too big for weak folks, and too deep for simple". The crux of the matter, as Cecil realised, was to make the right impression on the queen's mind. Hence during 1562 he put pressure on De Quadra's secretary Borghese Venturini to get him to reveal the secret association between his master and Dudley; while simultaneously Cecil stressed to Elizabeth the danger that the French Huguenots were facing from the Spanish-supported Guises. As he instructed Throckmorton in July: "Continue your writing to put the Queen's Majesty in remembrance of her peril if the Guisans prosper". Such were Cecil's preoccupations, yet when Parliament met early the next year and attempted to force the queen's hand on the succession issue, Cecil as Secretary could only play an ambivalent role. Although responsible for delivering the queen's carefully negative reply to the petition of the Commons, he concentrated his main parliamentary energies on delivering, in the words of a witness, "an excellent declaration of the great charges defrayed by the Queen's Majesty, and of the causes of the wars in France, for not keeping the edict there made by the Parliament; and also touching the charges made at Berwick Newhaven [i.e. Havre], the provision of armour and the navy, the cavillation of the French for Calais; concluding to consider for the aid". Cecil's dilemma was clear: at heart he was never other than loyal to the queen, and in public he must always appear her foremost servant, yet in terms of the utterly dominant succession issue his sympathies lay to a considerable extent with the queen's more footloose critics. No wonder that Maitland in Scotland was prompted to write carpingly to Cecil in 1564: "I have ever found that fault with you that as in your letters you always wrote obscurely, in private communication you seldom uttered your own judgement". Behind the complaint loomed the claims of Mary Queen of Scots. Few wished her dead more than did Cecil, but he came to realise with almost icy precision that he must wait for the decisive moment and not play his hand too early. By 1568 his policy, in its essentials at least, came to fruition: the saga of the investigation of the casket letters, Mary's imprisonment at Tutbury, and the recognition of Murray's regency in Scotland signified that Elizabeth had at last effectively turned against her blood relative. Cecil's steady eschewal of the rhetoric of crusade was vindicated.

The northern rising of 1569, comparable to the Pilgrimage of Grace in its hostility to *parvenus,* proved the point. This later generation of rebels also wanted to turn back the clock, but Cecil, like Cromwell before him, treated the issue far more objectively, as a military question of national security, and in so doing anticipated the modern concept of the "neutral" state. Cecil, unlike Cromwell, played a considerable and detailed personal part in the suppression of the rebellion, typified shortly before the rising began by a memorandum intended to increase the number of arquebusiers, preferred by him to practitioners of the longbow. In November itself, Cecil worked furiously to get the county levies into some sort of functioning order and also supported far more constantly than did the queen the under-supplied earl of Sussex, president of the council of the north. He insisted at the outset, moreover, that all J.P.s be made to affirm obedience to the Act of Uniformity. Cecil's reward for his endeavours came in February 1571 when he was created Burghley, only the fourth new peerage of the reign. But he remained for a time as Secretary, only formally giving up the office in July 1572 following the death a few months earlier of Winchester, the aged treasurer. Even as treasurer, however, Burghley continued to receive information and maintain a daily relationship with the queen almost as if he were still Secretary. When Walsingham was abroad in 1578 it was Burghley who stood in for him and also accompanied Elizabeth on her summer progress. While as Walsingham himself was to write to Wotton in Scotland in September 1585: "The delay of answer, which you desired with speed, proceeded through Burghley's absence from court". Indeed, with his son Robert installed in 1596 in the office, Burghley may well have reflected at the end of his life that the secretarial succession at least had proceeded relatively unimpaired.

The Walsingham Years: 1572-90

Burghley's immediate successor as Secretary was Smith, who during this second tenure of the office was little more than the treasurer's dummy. He wrote to Burghley after only three months at the job: "I do well perceive Her Highness is disposed to sign nothing except your Lordship be here". Smith himself disliked women, including Elizabeth, and had only gradually re-emerged into a position of prominence, culminating in the successful conclusion of the treaty of Blois earlier in 1572. But in terms of the highest honours he realised that he was a spent force. This seems to have depressed both his spirits and his health, though occasionally an old fiery flash manifested itself, recalling the moment when he had written to Cecil in 1563 opposing tougher laws against Catholics and sardonically remarking that "the hardest punishment for all papists by mine advice should be to confine them into Italy and let them live by sucking the Pope's teats". On the whole, however, Smith became steadily more gloomy during his second secretaryship. Never a courtier by temperament, he wrote to a friend in June 1575 that "this trotting about in progress makes many things to be unprofited and longer deferred than is convenient". Nor was Smith's humour helped by Elizabeth's refusal to back positively his novel plans for colonising and ruling Ireland, with the queen always declining at the last moment actually to authorise an expedition. Indeed, it was Elizabeth's almost catastrophic inability to make up her mind which especially dispirited Smith during his secretaryship. On 6th March 1575 he wrote to Burghley: "I can neither get the other letters signed nor the letters already signed sent away, but day by day, and hour by hour, till 'anon', 'soon', and 'tomorrow' . . . I would some other man occupied my room who had more credit to get things resolved in time". But by "tomorrow" things had actually got worse. Elizabeth was now refusing to have suits even presented to her and almost in despair Smith wrote to Burghley on the 7th that "we had need within a while to have a horse or an ass to carry bills after us". A year later Smith finally collapsed under the work-load with the additional duties imposed on him by the meeting of Parliament in the spring of 1576, though he remained nominal Secretary until his death in August 1577. A first-rate intellectual, he had been reduced in his last years to a life of pen-pushing.

It was quite different for the resilient Sir Francis Walsingham. He was appointed as the other Secretary in December 1573 on account of Smith's serious illness that month; and he was for much of the time during the next seventeen years to carry on, like Cecil before him, without a colleague at all. Walsingham was a born Secretary: a contemporary, William Camden, aptly described him as "a most subtle searcher of hidden secrets". Even before he officially entered the government's service Walsingham was providing Cecil with items of information about activities concerning Mary Stuart. His own persuasions were Puritan and he was, in Naunton's phrase, "one of the great allies of the austerian embracement". In office, however, he tended to moderate his convictions and, being particularly conscious of Elizabeth's aversion to religious extremism, was altogether more in the Cecilian tradition than is sometimes realised. As he declared in 1578 in a letter to another Puritan, William Davison, subsequently Walsingham's colleague as Secretary: "I would have all reformations done by public authority. It were very dangerous that every private man's zeal should carry sufficient authority of reforming things amiss". On another occasion and in relation to another theme, writing to Burghley in 1576 about the question of concerning himself with the customs, Walsingham affirmed that he would not "meddle therein" unless "I shall find her Majesty persuaded that I deal withal rather in respect of her service than of any profit to grow unto myself". Such professions of disinterestedness did Walsingham credit — though they by no means ensured him of a trouble-free secretaryship. To an even greater extent than Cecil before him, he was always seeking for a more

Protestant foreign policy than the queen would permit and only later on, in the aftermath of the Spanish Armada, did their relations attain any real warmth. A letter of lament to Leicester in July 1577 reflected perfectly the two central psychological motifs — desire and necessity — of Walsingham's period in office. The specific context was Elizabeth's refusal to give tangible help to the Huguenots under Henry of Navarre. Walsingham wrote: "This our art of saving twenty thousand pounds is accomplished with so many mischiefs like to ensure hereby as I fear will not be put off with the expense of a million. But seeing God doth not dispose her Majesty's heart so to judge of the matter, we that are her faithful servants must prepare our corselets and carcasses to sacrifice them in her service". In practice Walsingham did not always subdue sufficiently his critical faculties. In October 1579, after he had persistently expressed his opposition to the queen's projected marriage to the duke of Alençon, Elizabeth in effect banished him from court for the rest of the year. And Walsingham only kept his position on account of his consummate, incontrovertible ability at dealing with all the varieties of secretarial business.

From November 1577 until his death in June 1581 Thomas Wilson was Walsingham's colleague as Principal Secretary. His background was eventful: at Cambridge he had belonged to the Cheke group; in 1553 he had brought out *The Arte of Rhetorique,* to which Shakespeare is said to have owed inspiration for the character of Dogberry; during Mary's reign he had been imprisoned in Rome and had only owed his escape to anti-Inquisition riots on the part of the mob; and from the mid-1560s he had undertaken a series of diplomatic missions. Now, in 1577, he was reckoned to be the specialist on Portuguese matters, but had probably been appointed Secretary only because of Walsingham's temporary absence in the Netherlands. Wilson as Secretary was both hard-working and astute, sensibly toning down his Puritan instincts in accordance with Cecilian precepts. A letter to Leicester in 1578 about affairs of the council reflects his adaptability as well as his con-scientiousness. "Now the lords are like to tarry, I do think they shall have good leisure after the Irish matters ended, to deal with the riot at Drayton Basset, which is prepared and abridged for the Lordships to hear at all times with great facility". In terms of secretarial history the key word here is "abridged", given a heightened significance by the fact that Wilson as Secretary was undoubtedly subordinate in authority to Walsingham. Even under a relatively minor holder, in other words, the wide-ranging responsibilities of the office were beginning, if not to define themselves, at least to be assumed as a matter of course. Wilson accepted his junior role cheerfully enough: the two Secretaries had been contemporaries at King's College, Cambridge, and Wilson liked and trusted Walsingham sufficiently to appoint him executor of his will.

To turn back to Walsingham himself: he became during the 1580s an increasingly central policy-making figure on the council, but as Secretary the strains and problems of the position changed little. The queen's by now almost abstract pursuit of Alençon's hand lay behind Walsingham's complaint to Burghley in August 1581 that "I should repute it a greater favour to be committed unto the Tower, unless her Majesty may grow more certain in her resolutions". And in June 1582 he coined a memorable phrase when he wrote to Cobham that "providence is esteemed but prodigality and necessity is here President of the Council". The background to this particular grievance was peculiarly galling for Walsingham: in lucid analytical terms he had outlined by 1579 his belief that Scotland represented "the postern gate to any mischief or peril that may befall this realm", but Elizabeth still adamantly refused to give financial support to the more loyal Scottish noblemen as a counter to French infiltration. Moreover, though Walsingham did in the end receive partial satisfaction on the Scottish front, with the head of Mary following the revelation of the Babington Plot, the wider continental setting during the mid-1580s remained the continuing refusal of a part of the council, but more importantly the queen, to give muscle to the Secretary's anti-Catholic foreign policy. During the winter of 1586-7 he actually could not bring himself to stay at court. "Her Majesty's unkind dealing towards me hath so wounded me as I could take no comfort to stay there", he wrote to Burghley in December. Yet in personal terms his absence proved a blessing in disguise, as Walsingham, officially in ill-health, was perhaps not entirely unconscious that it might do. For in February 1587 Mary Queen of Scots was executed and one of the great set-piece scenes in secretarial history took place.

William Davison, appointed in September 1586 as the other

Principal Secretary partly because of Walsingham's faltering but not yet broken health, was a capable figure. He had had wide diplomatic experience and Burghley in particular held his organisational abilities in high esteem. Yet his bent of mind seems to have been pedantic, typified perhaps by his hobby of compiling Scottish genealogies, and in the crisis of his life he was found lacking in the necessary secretarial quality of flexibility. The ironies began early. In October 1586, in the overriding context of an imminent decision about the fate of Mary Stuart, Davison wrote to Burghley advising him that he and other councillors should persuade Elizabeth "to be more circumspect of her person and spare to show herself publicly than she does, till the brunt of the business now in hand be well over blown". Davison, a good Puritan determined that Mary should die, spent the next few months at Elizabeth's side trying to keep up her resolution. She at last stiffened herself early in February, but received no encouragement from her Secretary when she tried unsuccessfully to instigate an anonymous assassination of Mary rather than a formal execution. Consequently it had to be the axe: "the grief thereof will go near to kill him outright", Elizabeth sarcastically observed of Walsingham when she asked Davison to show to his sick colleague Mary's death warrant with the great seal attached to it. Thus the machinery was set in motion, the execution took place, and Elizabeth in a rage of remorse turned on Davison as the most convenient scapegoat. The charge against him was the pure technicality that he had not kept the queen's decision absolutely secret. Robert Beale, the clerk of the council who had actually taken the death warrant to Fotheringhay, revealed the political realities of the situation when he wrote several years later: "Mr. Secretary Walsingham was thought too stout, and would utter all. Therefore, Mr. Davison must bear the burden". Burghley seems to have been the individual luckiest to escape Elizabeth's wrath relatively lightly; and the mildness of Davison's subsequent personal fate suggests that this was generally realised at the time. Though he lost the secretaryship at once, he only had to remain in the Tower until the defeat of the Armada the following year. Moreover, his fine of 10,000 marks proved in reality a fiction and he continued until Walsingham's death in 1590 to receive his share of the secretarial fees. By the standards of sixteenth-century disgraces he had come out of the episode not too badly. Davison was a proud man, however, and his morale never properly recovered from the undeservedly malevolent nature of his downfall.

It was fortunate for England, barely a year away from the coming of the Spanish Armada, that Walsingham and Burghley did survive the particular squall caused by Mary's death. Queen Elizabeth was never in need of their services more than during the summer of 1588. They had for a long time seen the prospective danger and had put much thought and energy into making the nation's militia into a reasonably serviceable organisation. Obviously there were likely to be flaws at the level of local units, often impervious to centralising control, but Walsingham was not indulging in false self-congratulation when he wrote in December 1587 in a memorandum addressed to Burghley: "Through the chief care and travail of A. B. and C. D. [Burghley and Walsingham themselves] there was reduced into bands and trained in maritime and inland counties, under captains and ensigns, 26,000 foot and horsemen: a thing never put into execution in any of her Majesty's predecessors' time". There were certain differences of approach: in particular, Cecil as Secretary had been inclined to dispense with what he regarded as the superfluous habit of oath-taking at musters, whereas Walsingham, with his characteristic insistence on the unity of belief and action, made the practice compulsory. But between them they laid the foundations of England's internal military security. During 1588 itself Walsingham attained a pitch, even for him, of secretarial toil and commitment. His prime task was that of ensuring that the navy received adequate supplies, a difficult job logistically, but made still more taxing by the ceaseless uphill struggle which Walsingham had to wage against the parsimony of the queen. Howard, commander of the fleet, appreciated the Secretary's problems and wrote darkly to him on 7th August that he wished "some were of your mind"; while the next day Walsingham himself lamented to Hatton how he was "sorry the Lord Admiral was forced to leave the prosecution of the enemy through the wants he sustained". Yet despite the grave shortages of powder and shot, and of victuals also, the enemy was repulsed during these summer days, even though the victory could have been more decisive. Drake himself on 18th August paid his tribute too to the Secretary's endeavours: "I will not flatter you, but you have fought more with your pen than many have in our English navy fought with their enemies". It was handsome praise, but perhaps a commendation which Walsingham would have liked to hear even more was one less consciously paid to him after his death on 6th April 1590. One of Philip of Spain's agents in London wrote on the 8th to his master: "Secretary Walsingham has just expired, at which there is much sorrow". When the letter reached the royal presence, Philip could not refrain from writing in the margin: "There, yes! But it is good news here!"

Robert Cecil: 1590-1612

To the surprise of everyone Elizabeth left the office vacant after Walsingham's death. Essex tried hard to persuade her to reinstate Davison, who he presumably thought would contribute an anti-Burghley voice in the council, but as he reported back to the unsuccessful candidate, "in the end she absolutely refused to let you enjoy that place, and willed me to rest satisfied, for she was resolved". But she also disappointed the hopes of Burghley, who had hoped she might appoint his son Robert. Probably she thought him still too young and also was perhaps reluctant to put further power into the hands of a family that enjoyed so much already. Instead, she kept an open mind on the question, but turned to Burghley himself, inevitably, to fulfil the secretarial duties on an *ad hoc* basis. This is clear from the docquets covering the next six years, which record how envoys going abroad were to receive their due allowances "upon bills and warrants subscribed or to be subscribed by the Lord Burghley, Lord High Treasurer of England, as heretofore was accustomed to be done upon bills or warrants subscribed by her Majesty's Secretary". Although Hatton the lord chancellor wrote to Robert Cecil in July 1590 that "they all feel and know affairs are in good hands", Burghley himself found the additional duties burdensome and by January 1591 was grumbling how he was "roundly besieged with affairs to be answered from north, south, east, and west". Nevertheless, he doubtless appreciated the opportunity now given to him in his old age to introduce his son surely and confidentially to the intricacies of the secretarial office. By the end of 1591 Robert was a knight, a privy councillor, and in charge of a former concern of Walsingham's, the customs; while from about 1593 he became increasingly responsible for the secretarial correspondence. Though Burghley as late as the autumn of 1595 composed three detailed memoranda on the renewed threat of a Spanish invasion, at last in July 1596 Elizabeth took the plunge and appointed Robert Cecil her Principal Secretary. It was a well-timed move, for Essex, now canvassing the secretarial claims of Thomas Bodley, was still flushed by his Cadiz triumph. Of the new Secretary, Naunton again has some apposite words: "A courtier from his cradle . . . his little crooked person carried a headpiece of a vast content". Though his father's equal in statecraft, and his superior in literary style, there was a certain nervous edge to Robert Cecil's character that often made it difficult for him to bring the best out of colleagues and subordinates. Perhaps this was due to his physique: early on a nurse had dropped him and his figure thereafter was small and somewhat hunched. It was probably the only mistake made in his training to become Secretary.

It did not take Cecil long to assert his authority. "Mr. Secretary now rules all as his father did", a foreign diplomatist reported in 1599. And certainly his collection of offices was impressive: not just Secretary, but also chancellor of the Duchy of Lancaster and master of the court of wards. Between them their control over patronage represented an almost unopposable force. Essex above all found the situation insuperable when he made a final desperate attempt to supplant Cecil in the queen's favour. Quite apart from the blunder of the insurrection of February 1601 and Cecil's assured handling of the situation, there was never any chance that Elizabeth would feel able to dispense with her Secretary. Both politically and administratively he was irreplaceable. The well-known couplet that began to be heard soon after Essex's execution acknowledged the fact:

"Little Cecil trips up and down,
He rules both Court and Crown"

From May 1600 Cecil had had an assistant Secretary, specifically junior to him in standing, to help him execute his multifarious duties. This was John Herbert, a sound administrator, a former diplomatist and clerk of the council, and, most important of all, possessed of a loyal disposition. Contemporaries referred scornfully to him as "Mr. Secondary Herbert", but to Cecil he was an invaluable colleague who got through much of the more mundane domestic work-load as well as

being always available to go on particular missions abroad. Increasingly
Cecil needed such help as the pressures on him began to mount. When
the Commons in November 1601 debated in a heated mood the
question of monopolies, it was Cecil who bore the brunt on the
government's side. In his major speech, on the 24th, he promised
certain royal concessions, but went on: "I fear we are not secret within
ourselves . . . whatever is subject to public expectation cannot be good.
Why! The Parliament matters are ordinary talk in the street. I have
heard myself, being in my coach, these words spoken aloud, 'God
prosper those that further the overthrow of these monopolies, God send
the prerogative touch not our liberty'. And he added: "Let me give
you this note that the time was never more apt for disorder". The
effect was impressive and Cecil carried the day. But the undertones
were ominous: force of personality would not always be enough if
Secretaries who attempted to control the Commons remained themselves only the mouth-pieces of the royal will. Such a position,
moreover, demanded that the monarch trust the Secretary entirely.
Cecil only barely received this necessary confidence from Elizabeth.
She called him her "pygmy", but respected his abilities. Yet a terrible
scene took place during her last illness. After Cecil had told her that
she must go to bed, Elizabeth is said to have retorted: "The word 'must'
was not used to Princes. Little man, little man, if your father had
lived, you durst not have said so much, but you know I must die, and
that makes you presumptuous". As Sunderland was to discover at
James II's hands towards the end of the century, it was never too late to
fall as Secretary.

Cecil had his faults, but presumption, for all Elizabeth's rebuke, was
not one of them. He had taken elaborate precautions to ensure a
peaceful succession and in a series of letters personally dangerous to
himself had impressed on James in Scotland the foolishness of reaching
out for the English throne precipitately. Now, in the spring of 1603,
with the queen dead, Cecil got to know the new monarch in person.
They met at York on 18th April and in his slighting way James jested
that "though you are but a little man we will shortly load your
shoulders with business". In fact, honours as well as duties came Cecil's
way in the new reign: in 1605 he became the earl of Salisbury, in 1608
lord high treasurer. He retained the secretaryship, but increasingly

Robert, second earl of Sunderland.
*By permission of viscount de L'Isle, V.C., K.G., from his collection at Penshurst
Castle, Kent*

Sir Thomas Edmonds. It hath pleased Almighty God,
out of his singular goodness, to bring to light the most treuel
detestable practize against the person of his maiestie the
whole estate of this realme that euer was conceaued by the
harte of man, at any tyme, or in any other whatsoeuer; by
which practize it was intended not only the extirpation of his
maiestie and his issue royall, but the whole subuersion downfall of
his estate, the plott being to take away at an instant the king
queene, Prince, Counsaile, Clergye, Judges and the principall
gentlemen of this realme, as they should haue bin togither assembled
at the parliament howse in Westminster the 5 of Nouember
being Tuesday last; the meaning how to haue compassed so great
an Act, was not to haue it performed by strength of men, or
outward violence, for that might haue bin espied preuented in
tyme, but by secret conueying of a greate quantity of
Gunpowder into a vaulte under the upper howse of parliament
so to haue blowne vs all at a clap, if God out of his mercy
the iust reuenge against so greate an Abomination, had not destined it to be discouered, though very miraculously, euen some
12 howres before the matter should haue bin put into execution.
The person that was the principall undertaker of it, is one Johnson
seruant to one Thomas Percy, a gentleman
to Northumberland. This Percy had about a yeare a halfe agoe
hyred a parte of Wynyards howse in the old Pallace from whence
seemeth now, had taken his place of purpose to worke some mischeife
in a fit tyme: Hee is a papist by profession so is his man Johnson
into this vaulte whence had at sundry times conueyed a greate
quantity of powder, couertly filled some trough a barrell with
two small barrells, all which they had cunningly couered with great
store of billetts and fagotts on Tuesday at midnight, as hee was
busye to prepare his thinges for operation, was apprehended in the
place it selfe with a false lanterne, booted and spurred; there
was found likewise some quantity of small powder, for to make
a trayne a peece of matche, and a tynder boxe to haue fired
the trayne, when hee should haue seene tyme, so to haue found

nature, because I neauer sed nor heard the like in any state to bee
attempted in grosse, without some distinction of persons.
I do now send you twoe proclamations, and withall I write good to aduer=
tise you that this morning the persons named in it, being most of
them gentlemen spente in their fortunes, all inward of Poperye
& fitt for all alterations, haue gathered them selues some good
of fourescore or a hundred horse, with purpose as wee conceaue to
passe oure seas. Whereupon it hath bin thought meete in policye of
state (all circumstanc considered) to remit the Earle of Northumber
land to the keepinge of the Archbisshop of Canterburye, there to bee
honorablie vsed untill thinges be more quiet, whereof iff you shall gett
any judgment to be made, as iff his matie or his remouell, could
harbour a thought of such a sauage practize to be lodged in such a
noblemans brest, you shall do wel to supresse it as a malicious dis=
course, & invention; & as being onely done to satisfie the worlde that
nothinge is left vndone, both belonginge to vollicye of state, when the
whole Monarchie was prescribed to dissolution, & seing no more then
him selfe directly approued as necessary, when gerreaued the sen=
tence of the counsell for his restrainte. It is also thought fit that
some indiuiduall men should presently repaire come to those counties
where these recussantes are assembled to encourage the good, & terri=
fie the euill, in both to secure the Earle of Deuon is used, & remitt
on going forth for him as generall, although I am easilye perswa=
ded to beleeue that this faggott will be be burnt to asshes, before
hee shalbe twentye miles on his waye. Of all which particularly
I thought fitt to acquainte you, that you may be able to giue
satisfaction to that state, wherein you are. And so I remit you
to gods protection, from the Courte at White hall this 9 of Nouember
1605.

Yor verye lovinge friend,

Salisbury

Although all Ports and passages are
stopt for some tyme as well for Embas=
sadors as others, yet I haue thought
good to aduertise you hereof with the
speediest, rather because his Maty would
haue you take occasion to aduertise the
Archeduke of his miraculous escape.

Sr Th. Edmondes.

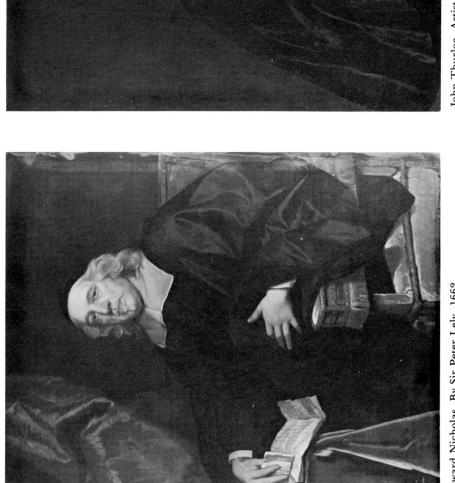

Sir Edward Nicholas. By Sir Peter Lely, 1662.

National Portrait Gallery

John Thurloe. Artist unknown, 1650-60. *National Portrait Gallery*

Henry, earl of Arlington. After Sir Peter Lely, c. 1665-70.

National Portrait Gallery

Sir Joseph Williamson. In the style of Sir Peter Lely, c. 1660-70.
National Portrait Gallery

James Vernon. By Sir Godfrey Kneller.   National Portrait Gallery

The cartoon is dated 8th January, 1641, and is in the manner of Faithorne. The other figure with Secretary Windebank is John, Lord Finch of Fordwich, Lord Keeper of the Great Seal, who likewise fled to France in fear of the Long Parliament.

By permission of the Trustees of the British Museum

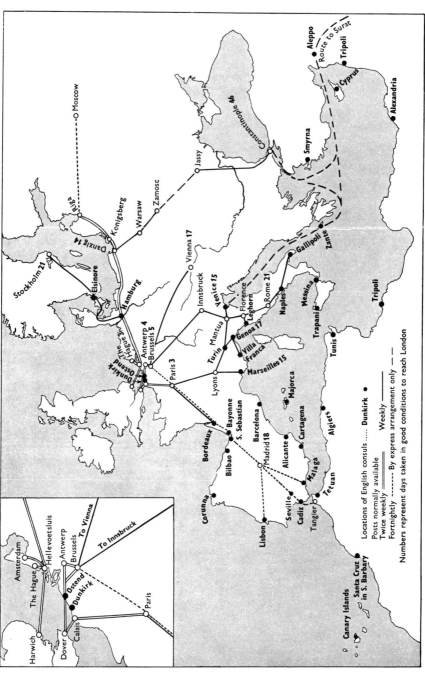

The location of English consuls, 1660-88, and some of the main postal routes used by the Secretaries of State, c. 1670.
From Fraser: The Intelligence of the Secretaries of State and their Monopoly of Licensed News 1660-1688. Cambridge University Press

delegated the routine administrative work, not just to Herbert now, but also to Thomas Lake, a clerk of the signet, and Levinius Munck, his own private secretary. Yet his day-to-day power remained apparently unimpaired. Francis Bacon noted bitterly on one occasion in his private journal: "At Council-table, chiefly to make good my Lord of Salisbury's motions and speeches". Gnawing away at Cecil, however, were his deteriorating relations with the king, of whom he appears never to have had a very high opinion. One story goes that he had piles of silver pieces left in a room through which James regularly passed so that the king might realise what it meant in real terms to dispense favours so freely among his personal companions. James for his part seems to have gradually lost faith in Cecil. At first he called him his "beagle", because of his ability to follow the scent of an argument, but increasingly, and especially after the failure in 1610 of the Great Contract, he tended to interfere in a pernickety, usually uninformed way with Cecil's work. Although as late as April 1612, only a few weeks before the Secretary's death, the well-informed Venetian ambassador insisted that Cecil "in spite of ill-health and absence governs everything", nevertheless it was a measure of his declining political hold that he was unable in the last years of his life to secure from James the release of Ralegh. One senses in this final phase a continuing respect towards Cecil as one of the great figures of another era, but a mood of almost open relief once he was dead. Or in the words of the uninhibited court verse of the day:

"Here lies thrown, for the worms to eat,
Little bossive Robin that was so great"

II. analysis

"How unpleasant it is to be employed in so unfortunate service I leave to your Lordship's good judgement".

The self-pitying tone is familiar, but what is noteworthy about Walsingham's remark to Burghley in 1578 is the degree of self-consciousness about the secretarial position that it implies. As early as the 1540s one senses this developing the close working relationship cultivated between Paget and Petre. A typical instance came at five in the morning on 24th February 1545. Paget, about to embark at Dover for commercial negotiations in the Low Countries, recalled at the last moment a crucial detail and instructed his clerk to add a note to the letter to Petre that had been drafted the previous night: "You will find Fontaney's ciphers among the other ciphers written upon, with Greek letters, Berthevilles cipher". It was Petre indeed who in 1553 became the first Secretary to be appointed by letters patent when Mary, on coming to the throne, confirmed his position. Although Secretaries continued to assume effective authority as soon as the signet came into their keeping, usually several days before they received their letters patent and were sworn into office, nevertheless here was a significant formal recognition of the secretary-ship's enhanced status. Under William Cecil, of course, the office attained its standing as a ministerial position of the first rank. Thereafter, until 1612 anyway, the eminence of the secretaryship held firm not only on account of the individual prowess of Walsingham and Robert Cecil, but also because of the absence of a lord privy seal between 1573 and 1608 and the further political decline of the lord chancellorship following the death of Hatton in 1591. By the 1590s, moreover, the Principal Secretary was beginning to be widely known as the Secretary of State. In November 1600 Robert Cecil wrote to Carew, the English representative in Ireland, about his new colleague and fellow privy councillor: "For as much as Mr. Herbert is now called to place of honour, it were not amiss that you do sometimes write unto him a short letter referring to the general, wherewith you know by his place he must be acquainted. This will take from him any opinion that you neglect him, and may prepare his mind to respect you hereafter, when peradventure death, sickness, or other accident, may throw you into his hands, as you now are in mine". And Cecil added as a footnote: "You may direct your letters to him in this form, 'To the Right Honourable Mr. Secretary Herbert, one of Her Majesty's Privy Council'". They are illuminating instructions: Herbert may have been junior to Cecil from the outset, but manifestly the office was now defining itself and in consequence forms of dignity were beginning to matter as well as the functional ability which hitherto had almost solely determined the secretaryship's rise.

Manuals

The string of treatises on the office written towards the end of the century confirms this new consciousness. Two such were composed in 1592, one by Nicholas Faunt, Walsingham's secretary from 1580, the other by Robert Beale, who, apart from being a clerk of the privy council, had also been Walsingham's brother-in-law and at least twice had informally deputised for him during periods of absence. Faunt's discourse is the less interesting, though its central point can hardly be over-emphasised. Namely: "Amongst all particular offices and places of charge in this state, there is none of more necessary use, nor subject to more cumber and variableness, than is the office of Principal Secretary, by reason of the variety and uncertainty of his employment, and therefore with more difficulty to be prescribed by special method and order". By definition, Faunt seems to admit, a written treatise can only be of limited value in laying down how a Secretary should act: the office is now far too flexible in scope to allow of purely theoretical guidance. Otherwise, Faunt says little, apart from giving a long list of all the books of accumulated information that a Secretary should have at his disposal and making the point, with implicit critical reference to

Walsingham's former habit, that it was unwise for a Secretary to have too many confidential servants in his employ.

Beale by contrast has much of note to say. While accepting entirely the intrinsic versatility of the Secretary's duties, his long essay, written on behalf of a candidate for the post who was eventually to be disappointed, is full of sound, tartly written advice about the practical aspects of the office and its political dangers. He makes the same point as Faunt about confidential clerks — "let your secret services be known to a few" — and cites William Cecil, who "had not above two or three", as a model example. When it comes to drawing up treaties in Latin, he advises Secretaries to call in "Doctors of the Civil Law and some discreet and well experimented Notaries", for as he adds: "Remember the saying of the Lord Hastings, Lord Chamberlain to King Edward 4th, in Commines; — That the Englishmen hath been more overtaken by the French in their treaties than in their wars". And in general, about the overriding need to know everything, Beale states flatly: "It is convenient for a Secretary to seek to understand the state of the whole realm". To help achieve this he recommends a reading, "although there be many defects", of Smith's *De Republica Anglorum*, written in 1565 but not published until six years after the Secretary's death. If these are all hints of an administrative nature, Beale is equally helpful on the political side. His tactical stress is simple enough: "When there shall be any unpleasant matter to be imparted to her Majesty from the council or other matters to be done of great importance, let not the burden be laid on you alone but let the rest join with you". Not surprisingly, Beale cites in this respect the unfortunate example of Davison. In terms of that often most invidious of tasks, waiting on the monarch, he advises: "Learn before your access her Majesty's disposition by some in the Privy Chamber with whom you must keep credit". Altogether it is a first-rate document: one senses in Beale's survival kit the very stuff of the secretarial craft.

An even more explicit Hobbesian fearfulness permeates *The State and Dignity of a Secretary of State's Place, with the Care and Peril thereof* which Robert Cecil himself composed about 1600. Thus: "The place of Secretary is dreadful, if he serve not a constant Prince; for he that liveth by trust ought to serve truly; so he that lives at mercy ought to be careful in the choice of his master, that he be just & *de bona*

Natura". In his characteristically lucid explanation of this nerve-racking dependence, Cecil incidentally stresses the integral part played by the Secretary in the conduct of English diplomacy: "Only the Secretary hath no warrant or commission in matters of his own greatest peril but the virtue and word of his sovereign, for such is the multiplicity of occasions and the variable motions and intents of foreign princes and their daily practices, and in so many points and places, as Secretaries can never have any commission so large and universal to assure them". It is a gloomy preoccupation, but Cecil's treatise is not entirely negative. He emphasises that if a condition of mutual confidence is to exist then it is up to the Secretary to play his part quite as much as the monarch. "A suspicion of a Secretary is both a trial and condemnation, and a judgement", he asserts. The treatise, moreover, is written with a delightful, even metaphysical, turn of phrase. For example: "As long as any matter of what weight soever, is handled only between the Prince and the Secretary, those counsels are compared to the mutual affections of two lovers, undiscovered to their friends. When it cometh to be disputed in Council, it is like the conference of parents, and solemnisation of marriage". He explains: "The first matter, the second order; and, indeed, the one the act, the other the publication". Even as Cecil wrote, however, the business of government was becoming far more complicated than merely reading out the banns to implement privately-taken decisions; yet the metaphor remains a useful reminder that by the end of the sixteenth century the Secretary of State was still wedded to the monarch of the day and thereby experiencing all the mixed blessings of such a dissoluble union.

Public Responsibilities

Robert Cecil spoke as a true Secretary when in 1610 he declared of long Parliaments that "they are neither good for the king nor the people". It was the assertion of a man whose belief in the royal prerogative was the cornerstone of his public life. In parliamentary practice this sometimes meant that as Secretary, trying to manage the Commons, he resorted to less than subtle methods in order to carry through the royal wishes. During the particularly vexed Parliament of 1601, with a member about to read a bill opposing monopolies, it was reported that "Mr. Secretary Cecil spake something in Mr. Speaker's ear", which he was well able to do since he sat in the next chair, and a few minutes later the Speaker abruptly declared the sitting ended. But the Secretaries did not always come out of the proceedings so unscathed. During the same Parliament, for example, it fell to Herbert to defend the indefensible proposition that the government could not afford to exempt the poorer taxpayers, since otherwise two-thirds of the usual revenue from taxation would go missing. Significantly, Walsingham as Secretary appears to have played a deliberately unobtrusive parliamentary role, partly doubtless because he appreciated the difficulties involved, partly because he was more concerned with matters of foreign policy, but partly also because he had ambivalent personal feelings about the relation of Parliament to executive authority. In 1581 he recorded in a memorandum: "If such a support should be required as might breed an open war between Spain and this Crown, then should it be very necessary to have the matter propounded in Parliament lest otherwise they may enter into some hard conception touching the same". No other Secretary of the period, however, seems to have shared Walsingham's rather advanced concerns. William Cecil was more matter-of-fact when he wrote in 1563 that "I am so fully occupied to expedite matters in this Parliament that I have no leisure almost to attend any other things". But for Cecil this process of expedition was a subtle one, full of deliberately blurred edges. In this he was different from his son Robert and in a long-term sense more realistic. His handling of the session of 1566 illustrates the point. While Elizabeth fulminated on how it was "monstrous that the feet should direct the head", Cecil concentrated on persuading the Commons to take off the pressure on the succession issue in return for his extracting from the queen the promise of a future marriage. As a governmental technique it was to prove viable for precisely as long as the monarch kept within certain policy bounds and the Secretary was entrusted to fulfil the demanding but still feasible role of honest broker.

The Secretary was equally the royal representative in a very special sense on the privy council. Both in drawing up the business for the council to consider and in putting its proposals before the monarch he was the pivotal figure, deriving his influence, it was understood, from his necessary proximity to the royal person. Potentially it was a role of almost limitless scope: Paget the Secretary, for example, who boasted of his intimacy with King Henry, was also the privy councillor who between May and July in 1545 attended 68 out of 71 recorded council meetings. In 1579 it was as if the earl of Bedford was consciously paying tribute to the Cromwellian revolution when he wrote to the privy council: "Some other matters of the state of this country I have imparted to Mr. Secretary Walsingham, wherewith I was unwilling to trouble your Lordships. If the same be of any value. I know he will declare them to your Lordships". And in 1592 Beale noted what had evidently become a firm habit when he wrote in his description of the council's procedure: "It hath been the manner that the Secretary should abbreviate on the backside of the letters, or otherwise in a by paper, the substantial and most material points which are to be propounded and answered". Moreover, the Secretary not only determined what the council talked about, but he was also an important agent in implementing its proposals once the monarch had approved of them. He spent a substantial amount of his time drafting the privy council's letters of instruction and was also particularly prominent on occasions of muster, mediating in often inordinate detail between the council and the recalcitrant county commissioners. He enjoyed, furthermore, a certain measure of control over the clerks of the council, who when at court ate at his table. Yet, obeying what one might call Beale's law, the wise Secretary still tended to shelter behind the less exposed authority of the council. Walsingham was especially careful in this respect and in 1587 suggested to Beale himself that in future he should address his correspondence to the council as a whole rather than Walsingham alone. Even Robert Cecil, politically the most dominant of all the Secretaries of the period, almost invariably added the rider that the orders he was issuing had the authority of the privy council behind them. With his instinct for self-preservation, he more than anyone knew it made sense.

Secretaries also tended to double as privy councillors when it came to the less wholesome aspects of sixteenth-century public life, which in practice usually meant questions of internal security. At its mildest this type of work might take the form of commissioning government propaganda. William Cecil, prominent behind the publication in 1563 of Bishop Jewel's explicitly Anglican *Apology,* was especially

active in this. Then there was the matter of censorship. In August 1549
Petre, Smith, and Cecil were instructed to inspect all publications
before they went on sale, but this was probably only a move of
temporary desperation. In 1597, however, Robert Cecil secured the
appointment of Bancroft as bishop of London and by that simple
device gained what was tantamount to control over the London
presses. But ultimately words in the sixteenth century counted for less
than deeds; and a far more challenging secretarial concern in terms of
internal security was the arrest and examination of suspects. In the
tense weeks of January 1603, Robert Cecil announced his intention of
clamping down on unauthorised travel when he wrote to an agent: "So
it is truly now so universal a thing amongst our English that have no
business in Scotland as merchants, no passport of councillor or
wardens, to go into Scotland, and of this no man feels the smart but
myself, all things being carried in another form when Mr. Walsingham,
my predecessor, lived". There is no doubt that Secretaries did have the
right, in practice at least, to arrest suspects; nor that they were
prepared when it came to it to torture reticent examinees. Even a
relatively minor Secretary like Sadler is known to have had a suspect
thrown into the Marshalsea, while the stolid Petre on at least one
occasion sharpened his attack by ordering the rack to be applied. But
as Cecil's letter suggests, the crucial figure in this field was Walsingham,
Secretary during the heyday of Catholic plots and counter-plots. In
November 1583 he employed to particularly effective purpose Norton
the "Rackmaster" on the suspect Francis Throgmorton. He confided
to a friend during a break in the proceedings: "I have seen as resolute
men as Throgmorton stoop, notwithstanding the great show he hath
made of Roman resolution. I suppose the grief of the last torture will
suffice without any extremity of racking to make him more conform-
able than he hath hitherto shown himself". Walsingham's confidence
was justified: one ordeal at Norton's hands had been enough and
Throgmorton submitted the next day as he was again being placed on
the rack. Such methods were neither everyday nor extraordinary.
Instead they were merely another technique to be turned to when the
Secretary felt the need to achieve a certain result.

Quite different from these spasmodic bouts of arrest-and-examina-
tion was the ever-present question of intelligence. Beale stresses in his

treatise how a capable Secretary must always have all possible information at hand in order if necessary to lay it at the council's disposal. And though the Secretaries themselves may have disliked and often mistrusted the spies in their employ ("I consider that those I use are but the sons of Adam", Robert Cecil once remarked), nevertheless there was no gainsaying the importance at this time of their function. Walsingham in particular built up a circle of informers personally dependent upon him and giving their news to no one else. He had always been hyper-conscious of the value of secret information, but it was not until the 1580s, in response to the spread of Jesuits and Seminaries, that he properly began to develop a personal agency of spies in England. Walsingham tended only to pay for specific pieces of information, of which one typical item came to him in April 1585 from one Thomas Rogers, alias Nicholas Berden: "The priests usually come over in French boats, coming to Newcastle for coals. They land either at Newcastle or near by. They choose this place because Robert Higherlife, the Queen's officer at Newcastle, is a papist at heart and his wife also. By his direction the priests with their books pass securely". It is important to stress the essentially personal connection which still existed in this period between men like Berden and the individual Secretary. At any one time other councillors were cultivating their own intelligence-gathering agencies; while Walsingham for his part did not hesitate to spy on his fellow-councillors, as when in June 1587 he sent off to the Netherlands one of his chief aides, Francis Needham, officially to act as Leicester's secretary there. In general the Secretaries had the advantage, especially after Elizabeth grudgingly began in the late 1580s to provide some £1,200 a year for intelligence purposes. The point came home to Anthony Bacon in December 1596. Faced by his Scottish correspondence suddenly drying up, he wrote to Essex, on whose behalf he was conducting a rival intelligence service to that of Robert Cecil, that clearly his agents there "apprehend Mr. Secretary's ambuscades and interceptions". Bacon went on: "They argue that if a public minister's letters to a king, his master, and the king's to him, have been laid in wait for, and opened, how much more letters betwixt private friends".

Domestic intelligence, however, was only a part of the story. The acquisition of news from foreign parts and about the key foreign

personages was an even more important secretarial task. William
Cecil, characteristically, had his doubts and feared being sold shop-
soiled goods. In 1567 he wrote to Norris, ambassador in France,
advising him to keep his costs down and explaining: "For at this day
common advices from Venice, Rome, Spain, Constantinople, Vienna,
Geneva, Naples, yea and from Paris, are made so current as every
merchant hath them with their letters from their factors". Walsingham
by contrast shed any qualms and during his secretaryship built up a
network which at one stage comprised over 70 agents spread around
Europe. Some were his own men, others were agents informally
attached to ambassadors, while still others were merchants and
miscellaneous travellers. "Knowledge is never too dear" was a favourite
saw of the Secretary's and beginning in the spring of 1587 he
performed a highly efficient job of extracting advance information
about the Armada. One of his agents, Standen, wrote a letter to
Burghley in 1591 that intimated something of the complexities of
Walsingham's method: "The year 88 which was the time that huge
Armada went and perished I was by his order at the Court at Lisbon,
where I had the view of all and by the way of Italy gave advice of the
whole manner of their designs, which by his letters I found in Florence
seemed most grateful to her Majesty". Beale likewise paid tribute to
the secret-service activities of his former master and advised Walsingham's would-be successor to employ a good spread of agents abroad,
though added sorrowfully: "But, seeing how much his liberality was
misliked, I do not think that you can follow the like example".

Nevertheless, it was beginning to be apparent, in terms of the
day-to-day conduct of diplomatic business, how the Secretary's unique
position in relation to his monarch would eventually lead to his
becoming Foreign Secretary as such. A foreign envoy in England
would almost invariably expect to treat with him; while in outgoing
terms, it was again the Secretary who enjoyed direct control over the
special posts and it was he also who was responsible for keeping in
touch with, and sending instructions to, the various English representatives abroad. When Walsingham was ill in January 1585 and it fell to
Burghley to draw up the detailed instructions for Davison in the
Netherlands, the treasurer scrupulously let the Secretary check the
dispatch, even though he knew they were in disagreement about what

its content should be. Each Secretary, of course, fulfilled in a different way his obligation to keep up the foreign correspondence. Smith, as one might expect, tended to be a shade harsh in tone and in June 1549 Paget rebuked him for his unnecessarily critical letters to Dansell in the Netherlands: "To say my poor opinion, it is good always to keep one word for him that is absent . . . men that serve abroad be best couraged". By the autumn of 1572, after a depressing spell himself in Paris during the 1560s, Smith had learnt his lesson. He wrote to Walsingham, his successor there: "I would not have you ignorant of that which I can show you. I know by myself how desirous ambassadors be to know what is done in their own country". Walsingham when he became Secretary was likewise generously informative; and so too Robert Cecil, who, it is clear from their surviving correspondence, kept Carew in Ireland well primed about what was going on in England and elsewhere. But Cecil was also a hard taskmaster: he demanded at least a weekly letter in return; he disliked ambassadors who became too intimate with the ministers of the country where they were serving; and, in Carew's obedient words, he believed that dispatches to the Secretary should aim "to advertise and not to advise". Clearly the whole business of conducting the foreign correspondence was a politically subtle as well as a physically demanding matter. Faunt makes this point in his treatise and contrasts the delicate foreign dispatches with the merely "consuming" domestic round of correspondence. Yet the greater problem for the Secretary remained not that of dealing with the foreign correspondence skilfully, though that was certainly necessary, but rather of ensuring that this control over the correspondence actually signified in a policy-making sense.

The Indispensable Secretary

Daily attendance on the monarch still continued to be the core of the Secretary's position, however much his public responsibilities began to broaden. It could sometimes be an educative experience. Beale tells the story of Henry cheering Petre up after he had been altering all Petre's drafts: "For it is I, said he, that made both Cromwell, Wriothesley, and Paget good Secretaries, and so must I do to thee". But as is clear from Paget's rise, and as must have been gallingly apparent to Wriothesley as his influence declined towards the end of Henry's reign, the opportunities granted by such constant proximity to the royal person more than outweighed any possible humiliations. William Cecil as Secretary subsequently perfected the technique of staying close to the monarch and taking all the really significant administrative decisions as an *ad hoc* committee of two. In May 1560 Throckmorton, ambassador in Paris at the time, lamented the imbalance caused by Cecil's temporary absence from court: "Who can as well stand fast against the Queen's arguments and doubtful devices? Who will speedily resolve the doubtful delays? Who shall make despatch of anything?" Walsingham did not enjoy quite the same authority, but as Secretary he was generally recognised to be the mediating figure between the queen and her multitude of petitioners. Even as prestigious a figure as Leicester accepted the fact when he wrote to Walsingham in December 1585: "Mr. Secretary: I have written a letter to her Majesty which I send you open, and if you think it needful, it may please you to deliver it". Inevitably, such a privileged position inspired widespread resentment. De Silva was probably accurate when in October 1564 he reported why Cecil was being sent on a mission to the Emperor: "I understand that the artfulness of his rivals has procured this commission for him in order in the meantime to put someone in his place, which would certainly be a good thing". Cecil naturally recognised the danger and at the last moment managed to get himself excused. His son was equally provident and utilised Herbert with this problem in mind. Robert Cecil was thoroughly conscious, moreover, of the need to establish a clearly-defined working relationship. On being congratulated in August 1603 on no longer having to get down on his knees as he had had to do when addressing Elizabeth, he replied memorably that "I wish to God that I spoke still on my knees". As Cecil implied, it remained as true as ever that an authentically strong monarch meant also a strong Secretary waiting by the side and ready to fulfil instructions.

In a financial sense an especially profitable aspect of this attendance on the Crown was the exercise through the signet of royal patronage. To take only the signet registers that survive for the period July 1540 to July 1541: during that year Wriothesley issued 586 grants of various sorts under his signet, Sadler some 329. Sadler's signet register also

contains an indicatively wide-ranging list of petitions that he as
Secretary must not forget to submit to the king's approval so that they
might be granted. For example: "The keeping of a lunatic to John
Peers. An exchange of lands for Sir Thomas Seymour. A grant of a fair
to the town of Gillingham. A denizen to be made of High Ryall Scott.
An office for my friend Richard Lyngham". During this period the
secretaryship continued to develop as a central source of quickly-
dispensed patronage. As one petitioner, addressing Robert Cecil in
1598, explained: "My state is too poor to let me await the uncertain
audience of a master of requests". Secretaries like Cecil have of course
been accused of deploying the patronage under their control with
private rather than public interests at heart. To some extent they had
no alternative: signet fees and assorted favours constituted their staple
income in the absence of a salaried bureaucracy. Moreover, there was
some substance to the contemporary charge that the Cecils in particular
favoured second-raters in order to reinforce their own position of
dominance. But patronage is not a subject about which one can make
easy generalisations. In 1602 for example, faced by the need to
appoint a new lord president of the Council in the Marches of Wales,
Robert Cecil resisted the insistent claims of Cobham, his headstrong
brother-in-law, and instead gave the highly responsible post to the
better-fitted Zouch. Moreover, whichever way a Secretary turned he
was bound to come under fire from those who had not been favoured.
Davison in the Netherlands reported to Walsingham in December
1586 that Leicester, leading the military campaign there, had been
complaining that the Secretary in England was not waving the magic
wand on his behalf: "I have done the best I can to let him [Leicester]
understand the hard terms you stood in almost the whole time of his
absence, and thereby yourself unable to do that you would, wherewith
he pretendeth to be satisfied". Undoubtedly one of the arts of being
Secretary was how to influence people without at the same time losing
friends. The cheerful response to Robert Cecil's death reflects the
difficulties.

The only sure thing about the secretarial income was the sum of
£100 traditionally received each year simply for holding the position.
Necessary augmentation came from the assorted and always variable
profits of the office, which were shared equally among the Secretaries

if there was more than one holder. Various estimates have been made
of the value of these perquisites: A. J. Slavin reckons that, quite apart
from the signet fees and the £100 annuity, Sadler as Secretary was
receiving at least £500 a year in bribes from hopeful suitors; but
Conyers Read puts a ceiling of £500 a year on William Cecil's total
perquisites, bribes included, during his first spell as Secretary. Certainly
it does not appear that the office became potentially a big money-
spinner until later in the century. In 1601 a contemporary put its value
as close on £3,000 a year. But in practice it was a fictitious figure, since
necessary expenses to be met out of the Secretary's private purse often
came near to cancelling out all the possible perquisites to be gained.
Robert Cecil complained in 1598 that "the direction of packets and the
account of them lieth heavy upon me"; and he added in the letter that
he had not been able to obtain recompense, for the expense was
"bitterly objected against me by her Majesty". Indeed, the Secretary's
allowance for intelligence had apparently dropped from £1,200 in the
late 1580s to £800 during the 1590s. It was never enough and by 1601
Cecil was again justifiably complaining, this time "how chargeable
and difficult a thing it is to maintain men abroad, as the Secretaries of
England must do". But at least Cecil had other irons in the fire besides
his secretarial revenue and he did not suffer the abject posthumous
fate of Walsingham, who left no money to pay for a proper funeral
and as a result was hastily laid to rest late one night.

It was a shabby reward for someone who, like several other
Secretaries of the period, had toiled with such single-minded dedication. Sadler's working day when he was staying at court is likely to have
been fairly typical: up by four in the morning and rarely in bed before
midnight. In July 1552 a dispatch addressed to Petre and Cecil jointly
had this apologetic note accompanying it: "As for the Latin, if you will
take the pains to read it over, if you have none other time to spare,
while you ride a-hunting, you shall well perceive that there hath been
much labour taken". Cecil indeed during his second secretaryship
drudged day-in and day-out with a zeal which none of his fellow-
councillors probably even approached. Characteristic was a memorandum of 1562 listing seventeen things to be done in the near future.
Some of the duties reflect Cecil's abiding attention to detail: "To make
exchange of £20,000 to Strasbourg to be there by the last of September.

To send to the ports for ships to transport soldiers and to Portsmouth to prepare victuals for 6,000 men for two months. To appoint skilful persons at Portsmouth to see to the speedy transportation of the men". Other tasks reveal not only his scrupulous care, but also his ubiquitous role in keeping the process of government in motion. Thus: "Sir Thomas Smith to be sent away. Letters to the King of Spain and the Queen Mother. The declaration to be published after the taking of Newhaven. Parliament summoned against All Hallow tide. Money to be borrowed before Christmas". It is easy to see how the presence of a Secretary like William Cecil, or successors like Walsingham and Robert Cecil, could become indispensable. A contemporary noted of Robert Cecil in 1599: "Mr. Secretary desires leave to go to Theobalds for six or seven days, but I believe it will not be granted, for he cannot be spared". Yet physical indispensability has never been the necessary precondition of great statesmanship: Bismarck and Gladstone, both given to long absences on their estates before making apocalyptic returns to the centre of power, knew that well. Algernon Cecil suggests the same point in his biography of Robert: "As one turns over the files of his endless correspondence the dim forgotten pleas of endless suitors come to seem like the wishes recorded on the *peau de chagrin* in Balzac's famous story, each of which is paid for with some partick of the man's ever-shrinking vitality". It is a convincing image. "God knoweth, I labour like a packhorse", Robert Cecil actually wrote to Carew in 1601. In a very real sense he and his immediate predecessors had been paying the price of the Cromwellian revolution. Cromwell had made the secretaryship into a first-rank office because he himself had been a superlative Secretary. On the whole his sixteenth-century successors managed to keep up the pace and be creators as well as executors. But once the Secretaries began no longer to match up to their responsibilities, then the secretaryship itself went, if not into decline, then certainly into a period of stagnation.

The development of the secretariat after 1540 confirms the decisiveness at the top of the personal element. Whereas the signet office declined by the end of the century into an existence of almost meaningless ritual, solemnly initiating the sealing process but useful only in the keeping of records, the corps of personal clerks attached at any one time to the individual Secretary became increasingly important.

The result was a curious admixture: clerks of the signet rubbed shoulders with personal clerks to comprise between them the particular Secretary's secretariat. The internal balance might change, and clerks of the signet increasingly delegated their numbing duties to men who could not afford to refuse, but until the abolition of the signet office in 1849 the overlap continued. Moreover, among the personal clerks themselves, it was not until the eighteenth century that there began to develop any general sense of departmental loyalty. Nor did the Secretaries themselves attain a bureaucratic consciousness for an almost equally long time. Boxall's thoughtfulness seems to have been an isolated act, since Beale subsequently noted that "of late years things have been made more private than were fit for her Majesty's service and no means used of instruction and bringing up of others in knowledge to be able to serve her Majesty". The fact that Burghley at the time was training his son to follow him as Secretary hardly weakens the point. And Beale adds darkly that "upon the death of Mr. Secretary Walsingham all his papers and books both public and private were seized on and carried away". It was a period when trust, the prerequisite as much as money of a functioning civil service, was in particularly short supply. In October 1559, with the French apparently about to invade Scotland. Noailles the French ambassador reported home: "In the management of this business they do not admit the presence of clerks. Cecil himself writes the dispatches and ciphers and deciphers those which are of consequence. The Queen herself, with one or two others at the most, frequently settles the most important pieces of business. Hence it is very difficult to fathom their proceedings". Obviously, only men of exceptional ability could go on operating at this sort of level as the problems of government became more and more complex. But while such men lived, then it was personality and policy-making that counted, not the development of still barely formulated notions of public service. In William Cecil's own phrase, a man without a friend at court was like "a hop without a pole". For some time yet Secretaries continued to look straight upwards and expected those below them to do likewise.

The Queen's Servant

In May 1572 Burghley expressed the main problem of his life when he observed privately that there was in the queen "such slowness in the offers of surety and such stay in resolution as it seemeth God is not pleased that the surety shall succeed". His devices to wrench a firm policy out of Elizabeth were several: memoranda that presented her with an overwhelming number of reasons to adopt a particular course, carefully-prompted reports from abroad to convince her of the threatened danger to the nation, and highly-coloured plots to frighten her personally. It was a shrewd technique, but it gained only the occasional success and certainly made no major long-term improvement in Elizabeth's treatment of her Secretaries. In July 1601, for example, Robert Cecil was almost counting his chickens too early when in a mood of much satisfaction he wrote to Thomas Windebank, one of his most intimate clerks and father of the future Secretary of State, how he had fooled Caron, the London agent of the United Provinces, in the setting up of an arms contract: "The Queen receives £5,000 of Caron, £3,500 of the City, and will only lay out £3,500 for furniture [arms] and £500 for victuals. Thus, she will gain £4,500 on this and every 1,000 men she sends". Yet the deal nearly fell through: despite the handsome rewards to be gained Elizabeth was unwilling to lay down the initial sum of cash involved, and was only at last prevailed upon to do so shortly before the Dutch became suspicious. It was a typical episode and Robert Cecil's gambits to deal with the problem were as devious as those of his father. As Francis Bacon, in his essay *On Cunning*, recalled somewhat spitefully: "I knew a councillor and Secretary that never came to Queen Elizabeth of England with bills to sign, but he would always first put her into some discourse of state that she might the less mind the bills". Nor was Cecil averse to operating behind the queen's back if it suited his purposes or, it should be added, what he believed to be the country's well-being. Increasingly in his correspondence with Carew, for instance, he insisted on receiving a secret letter for his eyes only to accompany the official dispatch. At the same time Cecil was highly conscious of the personal dangers involved in such furtive actions and indeed, during the period of his secret correspondence with James in Scotland, he became so security-minded that he sacked his private secretary, Simon Willis. For as Cecil subsequently recalled in a tone of deliberate understatement: "If Her Majesty had known all I did, her age and orbity, joined to the jealousy of her sex, might have moved her to think ill of that which helped to preserve her".

A general sense of anxiety could turn almost into neurosis if a Secretary was away for any length of time from the royal ear. Walsingham in Antwerp during the late summer of 1578 had a particularly hard time of it on several counts. His line of policy was rendered meaningless by Elizabeth's shilly-shallying; for the sake of the negotiations he lent the Estates £5,000 of his own money, but received no sign that the queen was going to recompense him; and he began increasingly to fear for his own position at home. In September; shortly before returning to England, he expressed his disquietude, probably to Leicester: "If it would please her Majesty to hear before she condemn, her displeasure would be avoided and her ministers serve with more courage and contentment. But I fear this mislike groweth by practice of some not the best affected towards me, whereof I have received very hard measure since my repair hither". Moreover, though Secretaries tended less and less to go on diplomatic missions themselves, the problem of remaining ultra-sensitive to the royal mood was bound to become still harder as the public responsibilities of the secretaryship began to multiply. With this difficulty in mind, and in line with Beale's advice, the Cecils used Windebank as their royal watch-dog at times when they could not be in the royal presence themselves. Windebank had been appointed a clerk of the signet in 1567, but before long became, in an entirely informal sense, something like the queen's private secretary. It was a sensible precaution, and doubtless sometimes helped prevent the Cecils from treading on thin ice, yet fundamentally the Secretary's condition still remained insecure. Even the mastery of detail by which successive holders of the office rose to the top could be a double-edged asset. As early as 1545, Petre in Calais was writing to Paget: "Because this matter be long and tedious I thought it not wise to address the same to the King's Majesty". Royal boredom, he was aware, could be as fatal as any larger policy disagreement.

It was not just the Secretaries themselves who were conscious of this state of dependence. Thomas Phelippes, perhaps the most assiduous information-gatherer of the time apart from Walsingham, wrote in August 1591 of Robert Cecil's prospects: "Some say the father is too wise to wish for him the Secretary's place, which is dangerous in the declination of a reign and in a doubtful succession". Possibly one can make too much of the interplay of personality and the causal significance of such a small thing as a heart-beat. Certainly the office did continue to develop considerably in public scope in the seventy years following Cromwell's death and the Secretaries themselves were at the head of far better organised secretariats than their counterparts in France. Yet the fact remains that the secretaryship rose in this period to the position it did — acutely described by Elton as "a cross between a minister, a high civil servant, and a courtier" — less on account of subterranean administrative developments than because, in a day-to-day sense, the thing worked. In this respect Elizabeth must take much credit: although she made life inordinately difficult for her Secretaries, she did perceive as no one had since Cromwell's day the potential of the office and ensured that the holder was almost always among her two or three leading ministers. It is merely a chicken-and-the-egg question to ask whether this would have been the case if she had not had men like the Cecils and Walsingham to serve her. The point was that the conjunction happened and hence stands as one of the great Elizabethan achievements.

CHAPTER FOUR

SECRETARIES OF STATE: 1612-88

1614 (29th March): Sir Ralph Winwood (died October 1617)

1618 (8th January): Sir Robert Naunton

1623 (16th January): Sir Edward Conway

1628 (17th December): Sir Dudley Carleton, Viscount Dorchester (died February 1632)

1632 (15th June): Sir Francis Windebank

South

1641 (27th November): Sir Edward Nicholas

1616 (13th January): Sir Thomas Lake

1619 (16th February): Sir George Calvert

1625 (February): Sir Albertus Morton (died September 1625)

1625 (2nd November): Sir John Coke

North

1640 (3rd February): Sir Henry Vane

1642 (8th January): Lucius, Viscount Falkland (died September 1643)

1643 (4th October): George, Lord Digby (resigned 1645, reappointed 1657-8)

Interregnum

1653-May 1659: John Thurloe

February 1660-May 1660: John Thurloe and John Thompson

South

1660 (1st June): Sir Edward Nicholas

1662 (2nd October): Sir Henry Bennet (Lord Arlington)

1674 (11th September): Sir Henry Coventry

1680 (26th April): Robert, Earl of Sunderland

1681 (2nd February): Sir Leoline Jenkins

1684 (14th April): Robert, Earl of Sunderland

1688 (28th October): Charles, Earl of Middleton (until December 1688)

North

1660 (26th May): Sir William Morrice

1668 (22nd September): Sir John Trevor (died May 1672)

1672 (8th July): Sir Henry Coventry

1674 (11th September): Sir Joseph Williamson

1679 (10th February): Robert, Earl of Sunderland

1680 (26th April): Sir Leoline Jenkins

1681 (2nd February): Edward, Viscount Conway

1683 (27th January): Robert, Earl of Sunderland

1684 (14th April): Sidney Godolphin

1684 (24th August): Charles, Earl of Middleton

1688 (28th October): Richard, Viscount Preston (until December 1688)

Stunted Growth: 1612-88
I. narrative

"Mr. Secretary has passed very well, having been sick only one hour last night at sea, but of other things you will imagine he is most sensible".

SO REPORTED an aide about Sir Francis Windebank's panic-stricken flight in December 1640 from Deal to Calais, a retreat from the hard realities of power which marked the nadir of secretarial fortunes during the seventeenth century. Windebank himself was merely one of a succession of victims at the hands of James I and Charles I, who both tended to choose second-rate men as Secretaries and expect them to act either as administrative hacks or political pawns. It was an era of soft-spoken favourites rather than hard-working councillors and inevitably the secretaryship, with its connotations of unglamorous toil, slid into the background. Indeed, following the death of Robert Cecil, James thought for a while that he could do without a replacement, though in fact Herbert did continue nominally as Secretary until his death in 1619, but seems to have been entrusted with little of significance during this last phase. Chamberlain the letter-writer noted in 1612 that the king was not hurrying to nominate a successor to Cecil, but instead "says he is pretty skilled in the craft himself and till he be thoroughly weary will execute it in person". So it was: the king's favourite Robert Carr looked after the signet (in an entirely *ad hoc* sense, never becoming Secretary), while James himself supervised the secretarial correspondence, though employing Sir Thomas Lake to take care of the menial duties. The experiment proved of fairly short duration. Councillors and ambassadors began to complain of the lack of attention and instructions they were receiving, while even in January 1613 Chamberlain was recording that "though his Majesty at first took delight to show his readiness and ability, yet that vigour begins to relent, and he must daily more and more intend his own health and quiet". Lake was left increasingly to his own devices and at last, in March 1614, with the Commons about to meet and needing to be persuaded to grant supplies, the king formally appointed a new Secretary.

James I's Secretaries: 1614-25

The man chosen by James was Sir Ralph Winwood, an honest sort of career diplomatist who now entered the Commons for the first time early in April 1614 and apparently remarked soon afterwards that the first speech he ever heard there was his own. His personal background was yeoman; and on one occasion during his secretaryship, he came into the council's chamber, saw a dog on his chair, hit out at the beast, and received the stinging rebuke from Francis Bacon that "every gentleman loves a dog". Nor was Winwood's secretaryship in general a happy experience. He came under constant sniping from courtiers who had desired the post for themselves and also had a rough time in Parliament, being unable to convince the Commons that all the king's "necessities" were in fact necessary; but at the same time he earned the displeasure of James himself by trying to persuade him that money granted for public purposes should only be used accordingly. James got on poorly with Winwood, a conscientious Protestant, and sometimes even tried to stay clear of him if he knew there were too many bills to sign. Winwood became still more unpopular in court circles when in 1616 he was largely responsible for having Carr and his wife put in the dock for the murder of Overbury four years previously. Such indeed was the strength of Winwood's convictions, and his hatred of Spanish Catholicism and all things to do with it, that it was he who also in 1616 secured the release of Ralegh from prison and secretly encouraged his plundering South American "explorations". The expedition cost Ralegh his life, as it might well have done the

Secretary's also, if Winwood had not first died of fever in October 1617, hastened it seems by precipitate bleeding on the part of the surgeon Mayerne. A few days afterwards Wentworth observed in a letter: "Mr. Secretary Winwood is dead, whereby you see Death expects no compliment, otherwise he would certainly have kept it at the staff's end with a kind of Hollander's austerity". One might add that Winwood's essentially low-lying, unobtrusive qualities had yielded but little purchase from his royal master either.

Seemingly more to James's liking was Lake, Winwood's fellow-Secretary from January 1616. A member in his youth of Walsingham's establishment, he at last attained the secretarial office after a long uphill struggle. A correspondent wrote to Carleton in December 1612 about Lake's high but vanquished hopes during the months immediately following Cecil's death: "Sir Thomas Lake had a commission to correspond with foreign ambassadors and keep them informed of all matters of consequence; this was thought a step to the secretaryship, but he assumed too much upon it and it was taken away". Indeed, it was in December 1612 that Lake lost his immediate chance of actual promotion. Performing the secretarial function of reading out the marriage contract on the occasion of Princess Elizabeth's wedding to the Elector, his French accent and standard of translation into English were so poor that for a time he lost all credibility as a potential Secretary. Lake took Winwood's subsequent appointment badly and caused a disproportionate fuss by claiming, unjustifiably, that half the Secretary's food and accommodation at court was due to him as secretary for the Latin tongue, a wholly nominal post. But eventually, as a faithful representative of the pro-Spanish group hostile to attempted parliamentary restraints on the royal finances, he did become Secretary in the formal sense. He does not appear to have made a great impact in the office, since after the death of Winwood, and until the appointment of Naunton in January 1618, James simply reverted to the earlier situation, with this time Buckingham instead of Carr looking after the signet and Lake once again being assigned the routine correspondence. Lake himself fell from office early in 1619. He had already lost the confidence of Buckingham after being forced to bribe him heavily not to reveal to James that his Secretary of State had rashly passed on to Suffolk some extremely critical royal observa-

tions about Suffolk's wife. Now an unsavoury family scandal proved
Lake's final undoing. The matter came to Star Chamber and James,
presiding, "spoke long and excellently to every point, comparing this
to the first judgment, Sir Thomas Lake to Adam, his Lady to Eve, and
Lady Roos to the serpent". At the same time, February 1619, Lake's
ignominy in being subject to this portentous homily was aggravated
when he lost his office to Sir George Calvert — though not until the king
had first verified that the incoming Secretary was married to a faithful
wife who had given birth to ten children.

   Calvert's fellow-Secretary until January 1623 was Naunton, a resolute
Protestant and far too upright in character to make much of the
office. As early as November 1596, as Essex's private agent based at the
Hague, Naunton had broken with his patron by writing that his role
seemed to him part pedagogue, part spy, and that he could not make
up his mind which function was "the more odious or base, as well in
their eyes with whom I live as in my own". He was of a hard-working
disposition and deserved his secretaryship, which in the end came
under the auspices of Buckingham. Within a year he was showing his
stamp and earning the compliment from Bacon that "Secretary
Naunton forgets nothing". The context was the odium quite unfairly
earned as a result of Ralegh's execution in October 1618 and the
widely-circulated remark of a rich City man called Wiemark that
Ralegh's head "would do well" on the shoulders of the Secretary.
Summoned to explain what he meant, Wiemark lamely said that what
he had in mind was the old proverb "two heads are better than one".
Whereupon Naunton, a commissioner of the fund for the restoration
of St Paul's, mildly expressed the hope that Wiemark might care to
double his already proffered contribution of £100. It was a well-taken
score and provided a rare moment of triumph in Naunton's secretaryship. Such was the hostile atmosphere towards him at court that his
wife even miscarried in trepidation after he had been berated by James
for entering into secret negotiations with the French ambassador. In
fact Naunton had merely been trying to improve the king's financial
position by seeking to extract from the French a dowry for Prince
Charles as well as the person of Princess Henrietta Maria — but such
was the secretarial plight. Naunton's effective end came in January
1621. Gondomar, the Spanish ambassador, accused him of opinion-

ating about James's most intimate dynastic affairs and Naunton was thereupon confined for the next eight months. In the event he stayed in nominal office until January 1623, when he resigned with little compunction, received a pension of £1,000 a year, and some months later became master of the court of wards. About 1630, with a rich if somewhat rueful vein of memories to tap, he wrote his *Fragmenta Regalia*.

Calvert's secretarial career followed a similarly frustrating course. He had been in Robert Cecil's service in the early 1600s and a clerk of the council from 1608. As Secretary he was very much forced to act at Buckingham's bidding and like Winwood and Naunton before him was not able sufficiently to bend his scruples to the prevailing wind and accordingly enter into the king's inner counsels. Calvert's role as the hack administrator was confirmed in January 1623 with the appointment of Sir Edward Conway, who had already been serving in effect as Secretary for several months, to replace Naunton. Conway's background was military: in his youth he had been a hero of the sacking of Cadiz and subsequently he had been for a long time governor of the Brill. He had not the qualities of a Secretary and was appointed as a pawn of Buckingham. "When your Grace shall think it fit to instruct my faith and industry, there is nothing so longed for as your commandments", he wrote to him in August 1623. Yet by staying close to the king, and leaving Calvert in London to fulfil the oppressive round of duties, Conway did in these early years of his secretaryship acquire a certain standing. In November 1622, even before his official appointment, Buckingham was writing to him: "The king will be glad for Conway to be at Newmarket to meet the Dutch commissioners and to bring his hawk with him". This role of being an old-fashioned court Secretary left Conway well placed in the winter of 1623-4 to follow the majority anti-Spanish line after the failure of the Spanish marriage negotiations. Calvert by contrast stuck to his earlier views and the two men became increasingly antagonistic. Calvert remained an honest patriot and certainly did not sell English interests to Spain; but in February 1625 he resigned, declared himself to be a Catholic, which he accepted was incompatible with his office, and subsequently as Baron Baltimore settled Maryland. The new Secretary was Sir Albertus Morton, an old clerk of the council who now bought the office from

Calvert for £6,000, which during the century was to become the standard price. A month later King James died and the good name of the secretaryship took a further turn for the worse.

Charles I's Secretaries: 1625-46

Morton spent most of his insignificant secretaryship undertaking a diplomatic mission to the Netherlands. He died soon after his return and was succeeded in November 1625 by Sir John Coke. The new Secretary was sixty-two years old, a veteran of service under first Burghley and then Fulke Greville, and since 1618 had been a not unsuccessful commissioner of the navy of mildly reforming inclinations. An honest administrator of small personal ambition, he was now too old even to take a Petre-like pleasure in his new responsibilities. Eliot was unduly harsh, but suggested the crucial lack of political imagination, when he observed of Coke that "his conversation being with books, and that to teach not study them, men and business were subjects which he knew not". Yet Coke held the secretaryship for fifteen years, notwithstanding the difficulties he experienced from the outset. Even before assuming the office he had earned the hostility of the Commons by acting as Buckingham's tool in the Parliament of 1625. Thereafter, in 1626 and 1628-9, it was Coke who bore the brunt of the opposition attacks as he sought to carry motions for the passing of supplies. Nor were his loyally Anglican sensibilities made much happier even when there was no Buckingham and no Parliament. He continued to be excluded from policy-making circles and during the 1630s came increasingly into conflict with his fellow-Secretary Windebank. Coke remained faithful to the king, however, and drawing on a lifetime's experience of diligent application on behalf of the government continued to operate on the sound secretarial principle of keeping his nose close to the ground.

Conway meanwhile had slipped into the shadows under King Charles I and in December 1628 left the secretaryship to take up the almost meaningless position of lord president of the council. He was succeeded by Sir Dudley Carleton, the diplomatist of long standing and high renown who had recently been created Viscount Dorchester. His lack of domestic administrative experience was almost total and, like Wotton before him, he does not seem to have had his heart in his secretarial duties. Dorchester tended inevitably to concentrate on foreign affairs until his death in February 1632, but found it difficult to counter the king's leanings towards the pro-Spanish group led by Portland and Cottington. This faction was strengthened by the appointment of Windebank, a clerk of the signet since about 1608, as Dorchester's successor. His appointment caused a considerable surprise and most observers attributed it to the offices of Archbishop Laud, who had taught Windebank at St John's College, Oxford. If this was so, Laud had misplaced his man, for as he admitted soon afterwards, "I have all fair carriage and all other respects in private, but in the public he joins with Cottington". It was true enough. Windebank may not have been an out-and-out schemer like Portland and Cottington, but he certainly had an unscrupulous streak and at the very least was concerned to make sure that his family benefited amply from his late promotion. Most of his sons finished up in his secretariat and Windebank himself, as a conscientious fortune-hunter, stayed close to the court and left Coke to keep things going in London. Before long they were consulting each other little and in effect running rival secretariats on behalf of rival factions, each competing for the confidence of the king. As early as 1634 a Spanish agent, Necolalde, was requesting Windebank to grant him a passport and expressing the fear that "Holland puritans" in the pay of Coke would seize him as he landed at Plymouth. Three years later Windebank was commanding Leicester in France "not to communicate this business to Mr. Secretary Coke, nor to give him the least touch of it in any of your letters". Their rivalry even extended itself to the question of postal reforms: Coke supported the ideas of Thomas Witherings that were aimed to give profits to the Crown as well as to ensure speed and efficiency, but Windebank attacked Witherings fiercely, as much as anything on the grounds of his social inferiority. The developing notion of the unity of the secretaryship, always a fragile concept in practice, was at this stage counting for nought.

The fall of both men illustrated in what a casual light Charles I envisaged the role of his Secretaries. Coke in particular was unlucky. Although his health was rapidly fading anyway, he was in the end effectively dismissed early in 1640 as one of the scapegoats for the disastrous First Bishops' War in Scotland the previous year. Yet Coke himself had been one of the councillors who, admittedly after painful hesitation, had come down against fighting the war. Edward Nicholas expressed the view of the more honest type of government retainer when in December 1639 he wrote to Pennington of the outgoing Secretary that "albeit I cannot commend him for anything, yet I wish we had not a worse in his room, for seldom comes the better". The end of Witherings inevitably came not long afterwards and he was replaced as postmaster-general by the rascally Philip Burlamachi. Despite this success, however, 1640 did not prove a good year for Windebank either. Oxford University pointed the way when, for all its firm royalist allegiance, it repudiated the Secretary as its member for the Parliament that was to meet in November and instead elected Sir Thomas Roe, a thwarted candidate for the secretaryship eight years earlier. Windebank knew, moreover, that he could no longer repose any trust in the king himself. The curt note addressed by Charles in York to him in London in August 1640, with the Covenanters advancing, was evidence enough: "I have nothing to say to you, but to conjure my Lord Treasurer & Cottington in my name to hasten monies to me". Windebank struggled during the autumn to redeem himself, but when his policy of releasing recusants for a fee rather than having them convicted got him into trouble with the Commons on ideological grounds (despite the fact that his motivation was strictly financial), he found he had nowhere to turn except abroad. "It is not in the wit of man to save Windebank", declared Hyde two days before the Secretary's abject flight in December. In fact he remained nominally in office for another year and even tried to claim his board wages during that period; but it signified little and Windebank knew it. Before his death in 1646 he only left France once, in 1642, when Charles in Oxford denied him attendance. Yet it is to Windebank's credit that in December 1641 he was able to write so graciously to his son Thomas in the royal household about Nicholas his successor: "For the new Secretary, it is a great comfort to me his Majesty has made so good a choice, and if I durst I would congratulate with him, but desire you as of yourself, lest anything from me be held contagious to do that service".

Windebank's colleague for the greater part of 1640 had been Sir Henry Vane, a wealthy, self-confident character in complete contrast to his predecessor Coke. During the 1630s he had held a succession of profitable household posts and he now assumed the secretaryship probably through the auspices of the queen. Charles at first welcomed Vane's air of bravado in the increasingly dire royal predicament, but their relationship was not long in turning sour. In May 1640 Vane made the mistake of offering to rescind ship money in return for the Commons granting the king twelve immediate subsidies. The Commons turned the offer down and Charles, who had probably authorised the ploy, characteristically blamed Vane for revealing how helpless his condition had become. But the central episode of Vane's period of office, the scenes at Strafford's trial, did not take place until almost a year later. The two men had been at odds for some time, an antagonism exacerbated early in 1640 when Strafford sought to have his son created Viscount Raby, despite Vane's proud first-generation ownership of Raby Castle in Yorkshire. Now, in April 1641, the Secretary took his chance and told the court the advice Strafford was alleged to have offered to the council in May 1640: "You have an army in Ireland; you may employ it to reduce this kingdom". Vane carefully advanced no interpretation of the words, but well knew how they would undermine Strafford's protestations that what he had had in mind was the reduction of Scotland, not England. Five days later Pym produced in court the notes which Vane said he had taken of that council meeting in which Strafford had advanced his plan. Pym had obtained them from Vane's son after the Secretary had foolishly left them lying round. On their appearance Vane affected anger and amazement, but convinced no one. It was obvious that he would wish to protect his professional competence now that he had achieved his main purpose, that of doing down Strafford and so indicating his allegiance to "King" Pym. Charles for the rest of the year was too weak to dismiss Vane, who for his own part was happy to remain Secretary and thus reinsure in case of a compromise settlement. In the summer Charles had no alternative but to allow Vane to accompany him to Scotland, though he not only ensured that the faithful Lennox (now Richmond) should act as his confidential mouthpiece, but he also informally entrusted Nicholas in London with the care of Windebank's signet and general watch-dog duties. By August Nicholas was complaining to Richmond that Vane had sent him "not a word of direction

which way or wherein to apply my endeavours to serve his Majesty",
though later in the month Vane did write to Nicholas, ingenuously
and not very helpfully, that "truly I know not how to direct you better
than to keep you in the same good way you are in". During the
autumn, as substantial moderate elements returned to the king's side,
Vane began to change his tune and represented himself to Nicholas as
the proponent of an honourable peace. But it was too late. Charles by
this stage knew his man and in the first week of 1642 dismissed Vane.

The king turned for a replacement to Lucius, viscount Falkland,
one of the most prominent of his recent moderate recruits. Falkland,
deeply unhappy about the imminence of civil war and only too aware
of the king's failings, accepted the office with reluctance as the
patriotic, potentially mediating course to take. After September 1642,
when he bore the royal overtures of peace that the Parliamentary
leaders rejected, his commitment to the king's cause became firmer,
but his hatred of the war lessened not at all. Finally, at Newbury in
September 1643, after at least one earlier attempt had failed, Falkland
managed to get himself killed in action. Clarendon (formerly Hyde)
wrote the memorable epitaph: "Thus fell that incomparable young
man, in the four and thirtieth year of his age, having so much
despatched the business of life, that the oldest rarely attain to that
immense knowledge, and the youngest enter not into the world with
more innocence". It was a fine tribute to a man possessed of an
integrity that made him perhaps uniquely ill-fitted for his office. His
belief that the spy was "a wound and corruption of human society" was
evidence enough of the basic incompatibility.

The new Secretary was George, Lord Digby, an even more brazen
figure than Vane, full of dash and improbable initiatives. Like
Falkland he had swung over to the royalist side in 1641, though Digby
now embraced the cause with a quite immoderate zeal. It is impossible,
however, to treat either figure as a major Secretary of State. During
the Civil War, with the acute constraints on the extent of royal
executive power, the function of the office was almost reverting to that
of the pre-Cromwellian Secretary: to stay close to the king and
personally fulfil his bidding. This temporary absence of wider duties
now permitted the office to be filled by an irresponsible and ambitious
favourite like Digby. Clarendon was probably accurate when he

described the situation that developed during 1644: "The King took the advice of whichever of his advisers he favoured at the moment, and Lord Digby altered inconvenient decisions to suit himself afterwards". The strength of Digby's position, in a purely internal royalist sense, was confirmed in the summer of 1645. Digby was in favour of fighting what turned out to be the battle of Naseby, whereas Prince Rupert was opposed; but after the defeat, it was Rupert who took the blame, not Digby, even though the Secretary compounded his error by losing all the king's correspondence during the retreat. But in real terms the defeat and its immediate aftermath meant the end of royalist hopes in England. Digby still had time to lose his master's papers once again, during a minor skirmish in Yorkshire in October 1645, but by April 1646 King Charles was in the hands of the Scots and secretarial notions no longer mattered.

But if Falkland and Digby are not particularly central figures in the history of the secretaryship, the same cannot so easily be said of Nicholas, who after keeping the signet for several months formally replaced Windebank in November 1641. He had come up the hard way: secretary to the lord admiral and subsequently the admiralty commissioners from 1625 to 1638, with all the tedious work concerning ship money that that involved, and also clerk of the council from 1635 until 1641 itself. It was not just his diligence and loyalty, however, which earned him his promotion. Bere, formerly Vane's secretary and now Nicholas', wrote to Pennington of his new master: "I cannot fail of good usage, and indeed his disposition is so sweet he is not capable of other". Predictably, though, Nicholas found life as Secretary extremely trying. He tended to be treated as an all-purpose donkey (a typical duty was making the arrangements to ensure the safe evacuation of the Crown jewels), but politically was sufficiently perceptive to feel persistent qualms about the nature of the advice the king was receiving. Nevertheless, his faith in the royal cause remained steadfast as first in March 1642 he accompanied Charles to York, thereby in effect surrendering all his own domestic possessions, and then in October 1642 settled down in Oxford for what was to be an increasingly irksome, practically unpaid stint of almost four years. Apart from attending to the royal correspondence when the king was in Oxford, his main task, in extremely taxing circumstances, was to act as a central royalist news agency. But his knowledge of what was going on was little respected early in June 1645 when, with the rest of the council left behind in Oxford, he urged the king to attack the Eastern Association. Charles and Digby, however, were other-minded and instead insisted on proceeding northwards. From Lubenham in Leicestershire, the king wrote to Secretary Nicholas on 13th June, the eve of Naseby: "I march to Land Abbey, after that to Melton and so to Belvoir. But I assure you that I shall look before I leap farther North. But I am going to supper". Disenchantment came swiftly and by the following year his most faithful of servants was beginning in France with other royalists a long period of dispiriting and often penurious exile.

Thurloe: the 1650s

Parliament was thoroughly sensible of the secretaryship's close ties with the Crown and as a result preferred to rely on committee rule rather than directly replacing the defunct secretariats. Yet committees need secretaries and out of this well-known conjunction there gradually emerged the particular secretarial pattern of the Interregnum. The key figure in this process of transition was Gualter Frost, an able administrator who became secretary to the committee of both king-doms on its inauguration in February 1644. Five years later, following the execution of Charles I, Frost was appointed chief secretary to the council of state at a salary of £730 a year. The job was one of obvious importance and it caused a surprise when, on Frost's death in March 1652, the council turned for a replacement to a complete outsider, one John Thurloe, rather than either of Frost's two assistants. Thurloe took his chance well. In December 1652, in addition to his regular council duties, he replaced the increasingly blind John Milton, secretary for foreign tongues to the council, as the secretary attendant upon the committee for foreign affairs. And in 1653, with the coming of Oliver Cromwell as protector, he attained a speaking as well as a recording function upon the council of state itself. With a king in all but name as his pole, Thurloe was now ready to climb like any secretarial plant before him.

The man himself remains a shadowy figure. His family background of a parsonage in Essex was ordinary enough; and little is known about his rise to the secretaryship of the council apart from the fact that he performed various legal services on behalf of the Cromwell family in 1650 and the following year reported efficiently on a diplomatic mission to the Hague which he had accompanied in a secretarial capacity. At some point Thurloe became close to Cromwell in a personal sense and he certainly played a leading role in getting his friend recognised as protector, being particularly active in sending off council-authorised letters to local sheriffs. Cromwell for his part undoubtedly appreciated Thurloe's clear, level-headed approach to business and also recognised that though the Secretary enjoyed influencing situations and acquiring a measure of enhanced personal status, he was not by temperament a man of thrusting political ambition. Indeed, though the evidence on the whole is lacking, Thurloe seems by the standards of the century, and the relative absence of grumbling by dissatisfied suitors, to have been more scrupulous than most in his transaction of public affairs. But can one simply see Thurloe as the honest plodding hack at Cromwell's side? Welwood appears to have implied so when he wrote in his *Memoirs* that "in matters of the greatest moment Cromwell trusted none but his Secretary Thurloe, and sometimes not even him". Certainly Thurloe's inability to impose his views in a decisive way following Oliver's death suggests that in a formal policy-making sense he was unaccustomed to taking the initiative. Yet to leave it at that is to ignore the entirely humdrum day-to-day base of secretarial influence. Lockhart, Thurloe's agent in Dunkirk, expressed the matter well when in October 1658, shortly after Oliver Cromwell's death, he nervously started a letter to the Secretary: "I know not by what preface to introduce a discourse of coals to your lordship, whose thoughts are so continually employed upon other subjects, but your lordship's care is universal". Or as General Monck had noted a year earlier, "I have already troubled Mr. Secretary Thurloe with so many businesses that I am ashamed to trouble him with any more". Oliver Cromwell himself recognised the solid authority which his Secretary possessed when through Thurloe he nominated his son Richard as his successor. And Thurloe it was more than anyone who was able to persuade Parliament that they must take the dying Oliver Cromwell at his word.

Under the protectorate of Richard Cromwell, who had little stomach for the job, problems mounted quickly for the ailing Secretary. In November 1658, after army leaders had expressed criticism of his corrosive pragmatism, he even suggested resignation. Things did not improve when Parliament met early in 1659. Thurloe introduced a bill officially recognising Richard as protector, but failed to prevent the Commons filibustering it out of existence. The effective end came in April when Richard, against the advice of Thurloe alone in his council, dissolved Parliament and by so doing virtually abdicated his position. Early in May the Rump of the Long Parliament was restored and, with committees once again replacing the central secretariat, the clock was turned back to the days of '49. Thurloe discreetly went into retreat, but emerged once again in February 1660 under the auspices of Monck to reassume the secretaryship as a suitable middle-ground figure. One John Thompson acted as his colleague, but this short phase ended in May with the Restoration. There was little chance that Thurloe would continue in office, for it was widely known that right up to March he had been trying to persuade Monck to restore Richard. But he escaped with his life without too much difficulty, being released from prison at the end of June on the condition that he be prepared to lend his expertise to future Secretaries "for the service of the state whenever they should require". It is not known whether these services were ever called upon before his death in 1669, but the stipulation alone indicates most strikingly Thurloe's reputation as a master Secretary.

Restoration Secretaries: 1660-85

Charles II had already made his first move concerning the secretaryship while still in exile in France. It is difficult to assess what his purpose was when he reappointed Bristol (formerly Digby) as his Secretary of State in January 1657, but in the event the appointment lasted barely a year, with Charles having the signet removed from Bristol's keeping following the discovery of the Secretary's secret conversion to Catholicism. Authentic secretarial history under Charles II did not begin, however, until after the Restoration, when the king appointed Nicholas and Sir William Morrice as the two holders of the office. Nicholas was delegated to take the southern department and be responsible for what tended to be dealings with Catholic countries, while Morrice in the northern department was to look to what were on the whole the Protestant states of Europe. Both men were to share as usual the secretarial responsibility for domestic matters. This division of foreign duties had in fact been introduced on the occasion of the appointment of Vane in 1640, but the circumstances of the time had given it little opportunity to develop into a coherent system. In 1660 itself the Secretaries appear to have been unmoved by the reintroduction of the division. Nicholas had celebrated his sixty-seventh birthday shortly before the Restoration and now as Secretary once again he found himself increasingly ill at ease amidst the lax morality of Charles II's court. His political significance lay as a follower of Clarendon, but in secretarial terms, to quote his biographer, "most of his work was nominal, only his signature and not his advice being wanted". Finally, in October 1662, he was pushed aside by Sir Henry Bennet, though Nicholas did receive £10,000 as the price of his resignation, a not unreasonable reward for his long years of service to the royal family. Morrice's secretaryship was similarly uncomfortable. He was never liked by the old court party for, quite apart from his prosaic Cornish gentry background, he had only obtained the position through being Monck's cousin and land agent as well as faithful parliamentary representative during the early months of 1660. Courtiers whispered loudly about Morrice's lack of linguistic expertise and from 1662 Bennet (created Arlington the following year) manifestly invaded his sphere of duties. Morrice longed to return to his home near Plymouth and his theological books, but was not able to do so until at last in September 1668 he successfully put in his resignation. To his credit he had not only lasted out eight gruelling years, but he had also complained about his plight perhaps more poetically than any other holder of the office. He wrote from his heart: "For though God hath called me beyond my expectation to a place of much honour and no little profit, yet contentment (the main roots of which are liberty and leisure) is a flower that springs not out of this ground".

Arlington was much more Charles II's sort of Secretary: cheerful, good at languages, a man of the world, and ultimately pliant. Contemporary estimates skilfully perceived his capabilities. Pepys described him in his diary in 1667 as a man who "speaks well and hath pretty slight superficial parts I believe". Evelyn was a little kinder when he reckoned that Arlington, though "loving his ease more than business", was "sufficiently able had he applied himself to it". But Burnet really put his finger on it when he described the Secretary as a politician who "had the art of observing the King's temper and managing it beyond all the men of that time". Arlington above all was the willing executant of Charles's foreign policy, though at times he found it difficult to maintain the necessary degree of diplomatic deceit without actually misinterpreting his master's rapidly-changing intentions. But he did his best and in 1670, following the secret treaty reached at Dover, Henrietta in her last letter to her brother King Charles specifically praised the Secretary as the figure most responsible for arranging the French alliance. Moreover, though Arlington may have lacked a sense of daily application to the more mundane secretarial details, his services at a higher level were ubiquitous. He it was who dispatched a yacht to bring back the Breton girl, subsequently the duchess of Portsmouth, whom the king had first spotted in December 1670 during the junketings accompanying the signing of the formal treaty of Dover. Indeed, it was Arlington who in October 1671 even provided his country-house near Newmarket for the consummation of the passion. Early in 1674, however, following seven increasingly uneasy post-Clarendon years of Cabal rule, Arlington came under direct threat when the Commons charged him on the grounds of papist sympathies, tyrannical methods, and unauthorised pro-French diplomacy. Phrases like "many and undue practices to promote his own greatness", "deceitful intelligence", "illegal imprisonment", and "a more than usual intimacy with the French ambassador" were indicative of the tone of the charge. The Commons in fact narrowly voted against requesting the king to remove him, but Arlington's political authority was now seriously undermined. In September 1674, in poor health anyway and weary of the continuing pressures of the office, he resigned the secretaryship. He became instead lord chamberlain of the household, though he continued for some time to be a significant diplomatic presence, even going on a mission to Holland later in 1674. His technical prowess in the field of foreign affairs remained unquestionable. But, as was to be Sunderland's experience later in the century, the fact was that once one had treated the secretaryship primarily as an instrument of faction, then it was no longer possible to enjoy the secretarial powers as an administrator if the political climate changed for the worse.

Meanwhile, in the northern department, Morrice was succeeded in 1668 by Sir John Trevor, an experienced placeman who had, however, performed useful diplomatic service in France earlier in the decade. He was the nominee of Arlington, who saw in him a willingly subordinate colleague and was probably not mistaken, for all his hyper-sensitive anxiety during 1670 about Trevor's non-conformist tendencies. In any case it proved a fairly short secretaryship, for as the countess of Huntingdon wrote to her son in May 1672: "Secretary Trevor died Tuesday last of an apoplexy, and Mr. Harry Coventry is chosen in his room. Secretary Trevor's death 'tis said was caused by drinking cold drink when he was very hot, and wine with ice". The new holder of the office, Coventry, took up his duties on returning from a diplomatic mission to Sweden and was knighted as he did so, the customary recognition paid to an incoming Secretary. He was a sturdy and honest character, who the king hoped would be able to appease the Commons and in particular the old Anglican Cavalier element. It was an uphill task, especially since Coventry neither inclined towards participating in the king's inner policy-making circle nor was himself trusted either by the Cabal or subsequently by treasurer Danby with the secrets of that dangerous, fluctuating clique. In February 1678 Coventry confessed to one of his staff the difficulty of being Secretary under such an incoherent method of government: "One day directions given here, and another day there, without adjusting or preparatory care, and yet much dissatisfaction if matters happen otherwise than well". By the end of the year he was badly gout-ridden and virtually out of action. Significantly, after some eighteen months in which no one proved willing to purchase the secretaryship for £6,000 from him, the office had to be given away *gratis*.

Possibly even more frustrated by the politicos was Sir Joseph Williamson, who took over northern affairs in September 1674 when Coventry switched to the more senior southern department following the resignation of Arlington. Williamson was the very antithesis of men like Arlington and Sunderland and anticipated not so much how the secretaryship itself was to develop in the future, but rather the embryonic permanent under-secretaryship. His background was fairly

humble — St Bees grammar school — and as Arlington's chief clerk,
and also clerk of the council from 1666, he cannot have expected in
the early 1670s to become Secretary himself. But as Evelyn graphically
explained, Arlington was so little inclined to burden himself with
matters of small import that in practice he "remitted all to his man
Williamson, and in a short time let him go into the secret of affairs,
that (as his Lordship himself told me) there was a kind of necessity to
advance him, and so by his subtlety, dexterity and insinuation he got
to be Principal Secretary". Williamson may not really have been so
deliberately scheming, but without doubt his omnivorous appetite for
work was unrivalled in the period. Yet, though a government man
through and through, his secretaryship was unhappy. He tended to
come under the thumb of Danby, who enjoyed keeping the Secretary
waiting an hour or two before seeing him, and also found it difficult to
discharge his parliamentary duties satisfactorily. The Commons disliked him and in November 1678, during the Popish Plot, had him
sent to the Tower (as a member of the House) on the charge of signing
army commissions to recusants. The accusation was fair only in the
most technical sense, and Charles had him released within a day, but it
was enough for Williamson. Three months later he ceded the office
without protest to Sunderland and, as befitted a man of his burrowing
type of mind, prepared to concentrate instead on bringing order into
the chaos of the state paper office.

The new Secretary, Robert, earl of Sunderland, was an ambitious
politician of swarthy countenance, well described by Burnet as
possessing "too much heat both of imagination and passion". Certainly
his first spell as Secretary showed all too clearly his impulsive
tendencies. He had received the appointment for several reasons:
because he had done well as ambassador in Spain and France; because
he was a confidant of the duchess of Portsmouth; and because Charles
envisaged that if it became necessary he would act as a useful
mediating buffer to the Country opposition in the Commons. Yet by the
end of 1680, though still remaining Secretary, Sunderland had come
down decisively, in his usual bullying manner, on the side of those who
wished to exclude from the throne Charles's brother James, the very
element whom he had been intended to placate into neutrality.
Sunderland inevitably lost favour with the king, but doubtless reckoned

that he had backed the winning side. He was mistaken. Charles
weathered the crisis and in February 1681 dismissed his renegade
Secretary from office without even permitting him to sell up. The new
holder was Edward, viscount Conway, a loyal nonentity who found
the position little to his liking and was well pleased when in January
1682 he was paid off as Secretary and put in line for the lord
chamberlainship. With Charles looking for an experienced figure to
execute his foreign affairs and still as susceptible as ever to the word of
his Breton mistress, back after a surprisingly short absence came
Sunderland, now a somewhat changed man. His abrupt and
humiliating dismissal had revealed to him as nothing else could have
that the Secretary of State still remained first and foremost the royal
servant, whatever his political aspirations. Indeed, until Charles died
in February 1685, Sunderland's self-confidence continued sufficiently
impaired to prompt him to play a low-profile role, simply making sure
that he did not offend his master. A new reign, he perhaps realised,
would bring new opportunities.

Sunderland's colleague for a part of both his secretaryships was Sir
Leoline Jenkins. His reputation was that of a stout Anglican of the old
Cavalier school, but his contemporaries do not entirely seem to have
had a high opinion of him. North described him as "the most faithful
drudge of a Secretary that ever the court had"; while Charles delighted
to play on his discovery that beneath the Secretary's upright demeanour
lay a secret taste for salacious humour. Yet it is difficult not to feel that
during his four years as Secretary, Jenkins was in the position of a man
of integrity, at heart a modest Oxford scholar, faced by impossible and
oppressive circumstances. From the outset he tended to be used as a
willing mouthpiece, being co-opted in April 1680 as Coventry's
successor in the continuing attempt to convince the Commons that
Anglicanism and loyalty to the rightful monarch were necessarily
compatible. Jenkins, radiating trustworthiness, performed the difficult
task to the best of his abilities. Whereupon Charles gave him as a
reward two distinctly unpleasant hatchet jobs: ensuring the appointment of compliant sheriffs in 1682; and supervising the subsequent
quo warranto proceedings that rooted out any further dissident Whig
elements in local government and also the city of London. Jenkins
disliked the work and mouthed ineffectual platitudes about the royal

prerogative being "best exercised in remitting, rather than exacting, the rigour of the laws". By April 1684, when he resigned, he was in a state of physical and mental exhaustion. In view of his belief in serving the monarch regardless of private doubts he was perhaps fortunate that King Charles did not die earlier than he did.

James II's Secretaries: 1685-88

James II's Secretary in the northern department was Lord Middleton, who had taken up the office in August 1684 after it had been held since April that year by Sidney Godolphin, the future treasurer. Middleton's family background was Tory, Anglican, and royalist, and he had just spent two years ably representing the Crown in Scotland. He was a diligent Secretary and from the first, even while Charles still lived, was regarded as a special favourite of James'. He also got on well with Sunderland, the two men sharing an irreverent streak. Middleton stayed for the most part in Whitehall and, though this meant that he did not attend several policy-making discussions at the formative stage, he certainly fulfilled his secretarial duties rigorously enough to ensure that he knew on the whole what was going on. For a time things went satisfactorily under James; and Middleton, describing Monmouth on the eve of the rebel's execution as "more dejected than ever woman was", was able to add complacently that "you may guess we are merrily disposed, and sure people never had more reason to be so". But as the Catholic emphasis in the reign became more and more preponderant, so Middleton tended increasingly to play a restrained hand. He eschewed all the secret dealings to do with Louis XIV and in the domestic field allowed Sunderland to impose his authority on all the secretarial tasks connected with the king's religious policy. The tactical evasion of responsibility was clearly becoming a more secular imperative than ever.

Sunderland himself was too intelligent to be altogether blind to the developing situation. Increasingly during the reign he urged moderation upon James, though to no avail. Yet at the same time he possessed such a strong psychological drive to be at the centre of things that he could not resist the temptation, in the context of James's dogmatic kingship and his own lack of religious scruples, to use the secretaryship in an unprecedentedly authoritarian, almost continental manner. A notorious example was the ruthlessness with which he carried through the expulsion of the 25 stubbornly Anglican fellows of Magdalen College, Oxford. Such an approach, however, made him even more dependent than other Secretaries on the good faith of his master. As Barillon the French ambassador noted, Sunderland sought "to reserve to himself some secret part of the King's confidence, by convincing him that he could have no attachment save only to him". And when James began refusing to take his advice about modifying his divisive policies, then Sunderland found himself isolated. The situation brought out the worst in the Secretary: following the example of Windebank, another abandoned instrument of despotism, he went into a funk. By October 1688, with imminent invasion a certainty, Sunderland was a tremulous and gloomy figure, given to wild speculations about terrible personal fates. On the 27th King James dismissed him. Sunderland may or may not have had the inclination to reflect for a second time that the personal touch remained omnipotent as long as a king was present to apply it.

There is little to say in secretarial terms about the last weeks of James's reign. Sunderland's successor was Richard, viscount Preston, a former parliamentary helpmate of Middleton's and of similar personal leanings. He had little opportunity to make his mark as Secretary, though he did attempt to persuade the king that even at this late hour there was something to be salvaged by adopting a course of moderation. Middleton meanwhile detached himself still further. Although he remained loyal to James and never envisaged serving another master (partly no doubt because his own wife was Catholic), he seems to have felt that the time was past when he could significantly influence events. It was a realistic attitude. The last days had their ritualistic aspect as Middleton faithfully accompanied the king back from Faversham to London after the humiliating failure of the first flight; but privately he expressed his relief when James at last managed just before Christmas to sail successfully to France. He desired a breathing-space and realised that with the abandonment of royal authority the secretaryship must by definition follow the monarchy into a state of temporary abeyance.

II. analysis

"Mr. Coventry has lately resigned his place as Secretary of State and I succeeding him in his Province, I desire you will let me know from time to time what occurs in those parts".

Thus wrote Sunderland in May 1680 to the consuls at Marseilles and Bayonne to inform them of his recent move from the northern to the southern department. The tone suggests a formally worked-out system, with the southern department being regarded as more prestigious than the northern and each having its own specific province of foreign responsibilities. Though in practice the situation tended to vary from secretaryship to secretaryship, on paper at least it was reasonably clear-cut. When Vane was appointed in 1640 he was charged to deal with matters concerning France, Holland, the Baltic, Germany, and Turkey. Windebank meanwhile, in what was to be the southern department, received responsibility for Spain, Flanders, Italy, and Ireland. This division was confirmed after the Restoration, though Germany was split north and south along religious lines and Barbary, the Indies, and Turkey were all assigned to the southern province. The authority of the southern department was still further enhanced in 1662 when, on the appointment of Arlington, France was transferred from the northern and Portugal, hitherto indeterminate, was added also. Germany, however, returned in its entirety to the northern province. It was in its own terms a logical enough system: one Secretary to concern himself with Catholic countries to the south, the other with Protestant states to the north. As such it merely recognised (with the temporary exception of France) the informal division of responsibilities introduced in the 1630s by the Anglican Coke and the

93

Catholic-inclining Windebank. It is arguable, however, that the departmental division of foreign affairs needlessly delayed by almost a century and a half the creation of a Home Secretary and a Foreign Secretary, instead of simply two Secretaries, which eventually took place in 1782. Right up to 1632, when Coke and Windebank began to play their rival games of acquiring foreign influence, there had been an increasing tendency for the two Secretaries to anticipate in an informal sense the far more practical division into home and foreign spheres of duty. Coke indeed between 1628 and 1632 had almost entirely confined himself to domestic matters while Dorchester, the veteran diplomatist, had undertaken the conduct of foreign relations. This is not to say, of course, that after 1640 one Secretary did not tend to be more vigorous and powerful in foreign matters than the other. But often this produced resentment and friction, quite apart from frequent misunderstandings, which would not have been the case if the more sensible secretarial division had taken place.

It is in this respect that the list of post-Restoration Secretaries is misleading. The appearance is of a minuet, a slow and indeed stately dance, with Secretaries moving gravely from one department to the other. Yet the reality was far different: a political rather than a stately rhythm and altogether messier. The question of seniority was always a major complication from the time that Coventry in 1674 went from the northern to the southern department and thereby broke the straightforward pattern by which the incoming Secretary, in this case Williamson, entered the department where the vacancy had arisen. The plum offered by the southern department was the French connection, the most important single aspect of English diplomacy during the period, but the imbalance it caused in the comparative status of the departments was often serious. It particularly affected the ambitious young politician who was forced to kick his heels in the northern department while perhaps a slow and plodding colleague played out time in the more senior province. Sunderland had especial cause to grieve when in 1683, on being appointed Secretary a second time, he found himself in the ironic situation of having to work under the same colleague, Jenkins, whom he had carefully chosen three years earlier as his compliant junior. An even more potent source of rivalry was the problem of overlapping that the provincial system inevitably created. No one thought of the division as utterly rigid and sometimes the issue was dealt with on a reasonably friendly basis. Nicholas in 1661 wrote to Turkey, where Winchelsea the ambassador was theoretically in his charge but in fact had been corresponding recently with Morrice on account of not hearing from Nicholas for so long: "Concerning the business of the King's mediation to make a peace between the Venetians and the Grand Seigneur, my brother Secretary tells me he hath written to you some time since his Majesty's pleasure therein, but what it is I know not, and shall therefore say nothing to you on that particular". Matters, however, were usually less harmonious. Morrice had occasion to complain that Nicholas had been keeping him in the dark about intelligence from abroad; and later in the decade he faced a sustained attempt by Arlington to wrest control over relations with the Low Countries. Moreover, the habit of maintaining a rival correspondence in the colleague's province continued as fairly usual even though it did not always produce acrimony. The secretaryship may have been one in theory since 1540, but it was to be a very long time before it became so in anything like regular practice.

Gradually, though, a certain secretarial consciousness was developing, as it had been doing spasmodically since Thomas Cromwell's time. Even before the departmental division of 1640, the Secretary based in London and essentially concerned with domestic matters had needed to have some grasp on events elsewhere. A foreign ambassador might arrive in London, the king might go on a progress and take the other Secretary with him, his colleague might even resign or die—all were contingencies which necessitated a certain degree of working collaboration between the two holders of the office. One such inter-secretarial communication was Calvert's request to Conway in August 1623: "I have at this instant received from you a new *réveille-matin* about the fleet, and would be glad to know of you in particular what I am to do more than I have done". There are other less tart examples: Vane and Windebank maintained a detailed correspondence during the autumn of 1640; Sunderland and Middleton kept close interdependent links in the 1680s. Secretaries were beginning, moreover, no longer to regard their papers as private property. By the 1620s the Commons at least was clear that such records should be considered as public in character. Indeed, in 1626 a Commons committee even searched the signet office for a letter, reputedly in the king's name, but which the committee claimed to have "pregnant cause of suspicion to be suppositious". King Charles predictably described the practice as "as insufferable as it was in former times unusual", but by the second half of the century Williamson, in his capacity as keeper of the state papers from 1661 to 1702, was able to build up a reasonably solid corpus of information and precedent left by departing Secretaries. Yet in inter-departmental terms there continued to linger an essentially private attitude towards the papers: Coventry in 1674 and Jenkins in 1681 both found when they took over the southern department that their predecessor had not left them the old foreign entry-book covering the province. The pattern of secretarial history as one step forwards and two steps sideways still persisted.

Domestic Concerns

Secretarial duties expanded in scope and to some extent answerability during the seventeenth century, but in their underlying character changed relatively little. Maintaining royal influence in the localities remained a major and time-consuming concern on the domestic front, as Sunderland's intricate preparing of the ground before the elections of 1685 indicated. But the dispensation of patronage—still in secretarial rather than treasury hands—had its problems also. As Conway explained in his deferential letter of August 1623 to Buckingham: "I have not time to clear myself to your Grace; but, thus, I am sometimes perplexed, not being able of your friends to conceive which is to be preferred". Middleton at the other end of the century encountered difficulties of another kind. Trying to persuade Captain Kendall, M.P. for West Looe, to vote in favour of a standing army, he asked him: "Sir, have you not a troop of horse in his Majesty's service?" To which Kendall replied: "Yes, my Lord, but my elder brother is just dead, and has left me seven hundred a year". But the giving out of favours could only go so far anyway in making sure that things went along smoothly. The good Secretary remembered his sixteenth-century predecessors and knew that the quality of scrupulous, unemotional vigilance was what counted in the end. Trevor learnt the lesson perforce when he was compelled to subdue his nonconformist feelings and root out sectarian dissidents in the eastern counties. Spies of course could play an important part in keeping the central authority continuously informed. John Wildman, one of Thurloe's men, suggested the dangers involved in his subsequent account of the work of his fellow-agents during the Protectorate: "They seldom or never came to Mr. Thurloe's lodging at Whitehall, unless sometimes in a dark winter night, for his lodging was constantly watched almost by all parties to see who of their brethren probably betrayed them". But though Arlington in the early 1670s employed one Colonel Blood as an informer on the Conventiclers, Secretaries tended on the whole to rely more on the traditional method of maintaining a voluminous correspondence with men of local standing. Such an informal technique remained heavily dependent on the energy, perspicacity, and good faith of the individual Secretaries. It was perhaps significant that when Sunderland in James II's reign tried to apply the more formal investigative approach he failed miserably. "There was never in England less thought of rebellion" was his considered opinion as late as 27th August 1688. Successful government remained government by consent, of the top few thousand at least.

Nevertheless, in several distinctive respects secretarial control over internal security tightened during this period in a more or less rigid way. One such area was the indirect but effective supervision of the post. Though Charles I and Windebank had thwarted the attempt of Coke and Witherings to put the postal system on a sound public footing, the modern centralised post office did come into being in 1660 following the Restoration. Parliament at the same time laid down that the Secretaries of State alone were empowered to authorise the opening of letters. It was a ruling of major importance, for though the Secretaries themselves tended not to take on the additional position of postmaster-general (with Arlington an exception), it was clear where the real power now resided. Thurloe indeed, even before the formal legislation of 1660, had characteristically gained access to the mail for intelligence purposes. His principal aide was Isaac Dorislaus, appointed in 1653 as "the Secret Man" to scrutinise the post from abroad and in the event holding the position until 1681 at least. He promised to Thurloe on his appointment that he would "manage that business for you with that secrecy and dexterity to your own heart's desire", but in practice, as Wildman noted, Dorislaus had so little skill in resealing letters that his transparent handiwork "caused great mutterings". It is uncertain, however, just how much the Secretaries after the Restoration used this particular prerogative. Coventry in 1677 wrote to the postmaster-general (still Arlington) that "the opening of letters is what no man can justify but from reason of state or the King's particular command", but it is impossible to relate the pious scruples to the reality. Certainly the powers existed — and what evidence there is suggests that the Secretaries used them fully as much as they deemed necessary.

The period also saw the intensification, in some cases temporary, of other secretarial powers. One Levin Brinkmary spent eight months in prison in 1636 on unstated charges as the result of a warrant issued by Windebank; and to an increasing extent warrants of commitment tended to leave the cause unstated. Moreover, in October 1661 a minor storm followed the revelation that seven prisoners in the Gatehouse, committed by Nicholas on the grounds of sedition, had been there since September the previous year. Such were typical instances, for though the *Habeas Corpus* Act was passed in 1679, the major legal campaign against the Secretary's arbitrary powers of commitment did not take place until the eighteenth century. Meanwhile secretarial control over the issuing of passports, safe-conducts and so on likewise became absolute. This was especially so after the Restoration, as the authority of the council waned, and passes even came to be granted to ships as well as individuals. But perhaps the most prominent secretarial powers of the century concerned the question of censorship. In 1637 a Star Chamber decree attempted to suppress unlicensed publications and in 1655 an order of council stated "that no person whatever do presume to publish in print any matter of public news or intelligence without leave of the Secretary of State". But the pivotal legal pronouncement, anticipating a far more ambitious censorship than anything hitherto attempted, was the Licensing Act of 1662. This not only stated that all books of public or historical concern had to be licensed by the Secretary, but it also gave him the power to authorise the search for unlicensed books and suspected seditious papers, in which capacity Roger l'Estrange was particularly active during the following two decades as official surveyor of the press. An especially harsh instance of the censorship in action occurred in 1676 when Williamson delayed the publication of Milton's treatise *De Doctrina Christiana* for what turned out to be almost a hundred and fifty years and actually had the original manuscript stowed away for safe keeping among the state records. The Licensing Act applied to newsletters as well as books and also in 1676 the government tried to ban the coffee-houses, proliferating rapidly as the centres of independent news. The attempt failed and three years later, amidst the uncontrollable flood of anti-government publications released by the Popish Plot, the Licensing Act was allowed to expire. And from that point onwards, though the Act was renewed from 1685 to 1695, the effectiveness of the censorship depended upon the varying will and ability of the individual Secretaries to do anything about the situation. The pertinacity with which the Whig newsletters kept going through the 1680s was clear indication that a more or less free press could not be long delayed.

These years of legal monopoly were not, however, without their positive interest. Williamson, in his role as the leading clerk in Arlington's office, was able in 1666 to bring the *London Gazette* into being and establish it (as Thurloe had done for a time with the *Mercarius Politicus* in the 1650s) as the only widely available publication that concerned itself with current affairs. Yet, because Williamson's primary concern was to acquire information rather than spread propaganda, there was in the *Gazette* a complete absence of significant domestic news. His reasoning was simple: since all such news could therefore go into the weekly newsletter sent out by Arlington's office to about 100 selected individuals at home and abroad, this would make the newsletter so invaluable that its recipients would pay in kind by sending back intelligence to the office. It was a policy which made for a dull *Gazette* and readers could be grateful when the odd account of a naval battle was included to liven up the pages. Yet the information provided was solid of its kind and people who needed to know what was going on continued to turn to the *Gazette* and the official newsletters even after rival sources of news began to emerge in the second half of the 1670s. Moreover, the hard-line distinction between the respective contents of the *Gazette* and the newsletter was additionally vindicated by the wealth of intelligence that filtered into the secretarial office during these years. It was a mark of Williamson's sound instincts that it never worried him if the newsletter ran at a loss so long as such key officials as postmasters, excisemen, and garrison commanders continued to pay for it by supplying prime local tit-bits. In retrospect, however, Williamson stands in secretarial terms as the last major representative of that almost obsessively ferreting tradition epitomised by Walsingham. The clandestine acquisition of intelligence was to change in style as a secretarial preoccupation with the emergence of party politics and less cloak-and-dagger techniques of upholding the central authority. The sour contemporary observation about Thurloe, that whenever he was in difficulties he pretended a plot, had in this sense a peculiarly seventeenth-century flavour to it.

Foreign Concerns

Secretarial responsibilities increased also in foreign affairs. Even when the Secretaries themselves tended to be of second-rate status, as was generally the case between 1612 and 1640, they were entrusted surprisingly often with the conduct of major and usually difficult negotiations; while after the Restoration, when the committee on foreign affairs was established, the Secretaries with their access to almost all the available information were able to dominate its discussions even more than they had done during debates on foreign matters previously conducted by the privy council. Yet, as Arlington insisted in his defence before the Commons in January 1674, the responsibility for all decisions concerning foreign policy was collective and never the Secretary's alone. Indeed, it was not unknown for a member of the committee on foreign affairs to go behind the back of the Secretary, as when in 1668 Bridgeman the lord keeper, thinking so little of Morrice, had Temple draw up his own instructions before he departed on his mission to Holland. And of course, before any orders abroad could be sent off, there was always hanging over the dispatch the need to obtain the king's signature. The extent of royal control over foreign policy varied, but it was often dominant and never entirely absent, as Arlington in his self-justification might have mentioned to the Commons if he had dared. Sunderland in particular, with his undoubted diplomatic talents, was to find himself under James II unable to formulate policy in any effective sense. One can, however, make too much of the implications of this type of constraint. The Secretary remained quite as much the king's servant as a responsible minister of state; and an opportunist holder of the office could still, as in Tudor times, make himself great by virtue of his master's authority and his own special position as the king's chief accomplice. Arlington indeed was defending himself in front of the Commons because such had been precisely the nature of his authority, the very reverse of responsible. Results continued to count more than constitutional criteria, as in fact they would even when the secretaryship became relatively more public and responsible than royal and private.

It is almost impossible to generalise about the work of seventeenth-century Secretaries in their capacity as effective head of the corps of English ambassadors, consuls, and agents serving abroad. These royal dependents, doing a difficult and often ill-defined job, looked to the Secretaries for instructions, reimbursement of expenses, and general encouragement. Often they were disappointed. Arlington in 1666 sent Aphra Behn on a secret mission to Holland, but she received such wretched remuneration that she found herself having no alternative but to pawn her rings. Sunderland's approach was particularly harsh, minuting on one dispatch his surprise "that any man should be so much out as to imagine a letter of his own from Prague should alter a resolution taken here". Sir William Godolphin perhaps best summed up the feelings of the isolated and neglected representative abroad when he addressed to Arlington in 1670 the softest of impeachments: "10 or 12 lines a week is no hard task, unless there be many ministers abroad, of whom you have more care". In fact Arlington's office was at the time in correspondence with some 54 men abroad and increasingly tended, under Williamson's immediate auspices, to send the weekly newsletter rather than individually-tailored but often overlapping dispatches on occasions when there were no specific directives to issue. It was no doubt a necessary device in a time-and-motion sense, but perhaps mistaken. The personal relationship between the envoy and the Secretary continued to determine the quality and value of the correspondence, as it had during the sixteenth century or when in February 1641 one of Windebank's former representatives wrote to a friend scorning "the little ex-secretarius" and asserting "I never held any other correspondence with him, heretofore, than that which his office and my employment required". But though a strong personal connection was indispensable, as much in the 1670s when treasurer Danby was keeping up a detailed correspondence with the representatives abroad as during the Buckingham era, it had its inherent defects, like any exercise of patronage. "How little we are sensible of the weight of the business upon us", commented Pepys in his diary in 1666 following the appointment of the wholly inexperienced Nicholas Morrice, the Secretary's son, as secretary to the embassy to Breda. Nevertheless, if the age of professional diplomacy had not yet come, there was still a certain amount of sound, even generous guidance exercised during the period by the Secretaries, often with diplomatic experience themselves. Winwood when he became Secretary asked Trumbull in Brussels to pass on secretly any ill talk he heard concerning King James, but at the same time advised him that he should not in his dispatches to the king himself make reference to "any disgraceful or contemptible speeches they use against him". Over half a century later, following the death of the duke of Richmond on service in Denmark, Secretary Coventry broke the no-reimbursement rule for passages home by permitting as "just and reasonable" an allowance for the body to be brought back to England. It was not perhaps a gesture of remarkable liberality, but it was more than several other holders of the office would have considered proper.

The acquisition of foreign intelligence from these representatives abroad remained a matter of fundamental importance and continued to pose the same basic problem for seventeenth-century Secretaries that it had once done for William Cecil. Sunderland by the 1680s was receiving about £3,000 a year for intelligence purposes, but even that was not sufficient. On one occasion, after writing with characteristic rudeness to Savile in France that "your intelligences are the worst informed in the world, no one word of having been ever spoke of like what you mention", he received from Savile a simple and unanswerable reply: "There is nothing so easy as to furnish you with men who shall send you the ordinary occurrences which are only the materials of a Gazette. But for things more difficult and necessary to be known, it will be hard to find a fit instrument, and when found, are not to be gained but by such temptations as would perhaps be above your reach,

for that ware would be sold by small parcels and at great rates".
Nevertheless, though the problem was perennial, there did take place
from the 1650s, following a certain rustiness after Robert Cecil's time,
a revival in secretarial methods of rooting out foreign plans and
movements. The key figure was Thurloe, who spent so much of his
secretaryship successfully exposing plots that, as Henry Cromwell once
remarked to him, "really, it is a wonder you can pick so many locks
leading into the hearts of wicked men as you do". It is possible,
however, that in this respect Thurloe has been overrated, both as an
interceptor and decipherer of royalist communications and as an
extractor of foreign intelligence. Significantly, it was Arlington rather
than Thurloe who seems to have first used consuls in a systematic way
as providers of information disguised as trading representatives at
foreign ports. But later in the 1660s it was Arlington and to a lesser
extent Morrice who took the blame in a secretarial *cause célèbre* that
was partly responsible for Thurloe's subsequent high reputation in the
field of foreign intelligence.

The background to the episode was the division of the English fleet
late in May 1666 and the disastrous Four Days' Battle with the Dutch
which followed immediately afterwards. When the resultant committee
of inquiry eventually reported to the Commons, in February 1668, it
flatly condemned the Secretaries for the "want of intelligence from
abroad" that had allowed the fateful division to take place. The
Secretaries were asked to account for themselves and Morrice complained that they could not hope to provide a better service unless they
received an allowance for intelligence comparable to Thurloe's.
Whereupon Andrew Marvell, Thurloe's old aide, wryly observed: 'We
have had Bristols and Cecils Secretaries, and by them knew the King of
Spain's junto, and letters of the Pope's cabinet; and now such a strange
account of things! The money allowed for intelligence so small the
intelligence was accordingly . . ." It was hardly a fair rejoinder, but
tellingly ironic. Morrice, however, was a less central target of the
Commons than Arlington, who, because he had been in bed at the
crucial moment, had failed to countersign in time the orders necessary
to ensure a united fleet. Even less reasonable as a charge against
Arlington was that levelled by the naval commander Albemarle
(formerly Monck) soon after the defeat that he had been left in

ignorance about the movements of the Dutch. It was a wholly inappropriate accusation, for every reader of the *London Gazette* during May 1666 was aware that the Dutch had successfully gathered off Texel and were ready for action. A likely explanation for the trumped-up victimisation which ensued is twofold: partly it was a question of Clarendon fearing Arlington and managing to get Albemarle and the other naval commander Prince Rupert to put the blame firmly on his rival; and partly it was the usual case of the Secretaries being assigned the scapegoat role following a setback. Certainly the whole affair dampened the aspirations of Sir William Coventry, who was talked about during 1667 as a likely successor to Morrice but as secretary to the duke of York, the lord high admiral, had been implicated. Pepys in October 1667 recorded Coventry's thoughts about the possibility of assuming the office: "He would not by any means now take it, if given him, nor anything but in commission with others who may bear part of the blame".

The Secretary as Councillor

The Secretary's unique relationship with the privy council continued in the seventeenth century to play a large part in maintaining and developing the office's pervasive everyday influence. Even when Buckingham was controlling affairs in the 1620s the Secretaries still had much to do in ensuring the smooth working of not only the council itself but also its several and diverse committees. During the century the office of lord president of the council was periodically in abeyance and an order of 1628 formally confirmed the practice concerning council procedure already effectively established by the Tudor Secretaries. Namely, on the assumption the lord president was absent: "If any of the Principal Secretaries have anything to deliver from the king or of other intelligence, this is to be done by the Principal Secretary standing at the upper end of the board, and when he hath put the business in a way, then he is to go back and take his own place". The implications of this directive were necessarily open-ended and the cautious Secretary continued to put as much or as little weight on his conciliar responsibilities as seemed desirable in the particular circumstances. When in October 1681 members of the council criticised the Secretaries for not presenting them earlier with an important item of information that had suddenly come up in the course of the discussion, Jenkins was able to reply ingenuously that "it was the duty of the Secretaries to manage those correspondencies that his Majesty should direct that he should have a constant and punctual account of it, but that they were not at liberty to carry any part of their intelligences to the council, unless his Majesty directed it specially to be done". It was a deft but unconvincing disclaimer, for in effective terms the Secretary was undoubtedly (if he had the personal strength to carry it) dominant and indispensable. Constant attendance remained the fundamental prerequisite, especially with the proliferation of committees of council following the Restoration. Between 1660 and 1664, indeed, the Secretaries were members of no less than 47 of these committees, while Clarendon as chancellor participated in only 17. The secretaryship may still have lacked a certain prestige, but much more to the point was that it had access to almost all the vital information, above all through its control directly over intelligence and indirectly over Crown patronage. In possession of such an advantage, even a second-rate Secretary was always going to be significant in a day-to-day sense and as a result could not fail to influence policy to at least some extent.

An example of this was the Secretary's fluctuating importance in military matters. He could never be entirely ruled out on account of his permanent double role as the Crown's intermediary in the making of military appointments and the sender of council orders to officers, but at the more decisive level of operations everything depended on the circumstances and the particular qualities of the Secretary. Conway and Coke in the 1620s revived the Walsingham era with a new and intensive round of military and naval memoranda, but they were very much the exceptions until first Digby and then Thurloe utilised the emergency conditions of their time to their own advantage. This was especially so in the case of Thurloe, who was so ready to issue detailed orders that he has been aptly described* as "the second-in-command in a military state". The Secretaries continued to be active in a military sense during Charles II's reign, as when in May 1667 Arlington directed the lords lieutenant to liaise with their local militia and added the note "horse being the force that must discourage the enemy from landing" as a reference to the run-down state of the navy. Moreover, though Arlington accepted in the early 1670s that actual command of

*Florence M. Greir Evans, *The Principal Secretary of State* (1923), p. 117.

the army lay with the commander-in-chief, the duke of Monmouth, he never at any stage allowed the appointing process to pass out of his hands. This was unfortunately not so in the case of Williamson, who in reality was acting under Monmouth's orders when in 1678 he signed the recusant commissions. Monmouth, however, fell the following year and Sunderland as Secretary assumed effective control over the army until the appointment in 1683 of William Blathwayt as secretary at war. It was an early indication of that dividing of the arms of government which in time inevitably deprived the Secretary of State of much of his omnicompetence. But he was not to go down without a struggle, least of all in the military sphere.

Naval affairs (Coke notwithstanding) constituted a less prominent secretarial activity during the period. In an active everyday sense the Secretaries tended only to interfere with the admiralty if a voyage or manoeuvre appeared likely to have diplomatic implications. The Dutch Wars entwined naval and political considerations in a particularly complex way; and Arlington enjoyed sufficient directive authority to cause Admiral Holmes to rebuke him in March 1672, shortly before the Third War, for his indecisiveness in ordering the seizure of all possible Dutch ships. "You have let slip the best opportunity that ever people had to destroy those I think you will make your enemies" were the admiral's unequivocal words, for all the tactful deference of the "I think". In general, though, it was the usual conjunction of personality and circumstance that determined the strength of the secretarial presence in naval affairs. The same was equally true of Irish and colonial affairs, both of which after the Restoration became the responsibility of standing committees of council rather than the council as such, though both continued to be subject to the varying influence of the Secretaries on account of their leading role on those committees. In Irish affairs the Secretary possessed the additional advantage of being the official middle-man in all communications between the king and the lord lieutenant in Ireland itself. As for colonial matters, this was such a nascent and therefore scarcely defined field of activity that it proved particularly damaging to inter-secretarial relations. "For the ill blood it may cause, it may be it was not the least of his design", wrote Windebank in 1639 about an order of Coke to do with plantations in America that had only come to Windebank's attention after it had been issued. The order, Windebank concluded significantly, "was never well digested in council, which, considering the weight and consequence of it, should most necessarily have been done". The situation remained fluid and potentially abrasive even after the establishment of the committee for trade and plantations early in Charles II's reign. Coventry was only guarding against obvious dangers when on one occasion he sent an accompanying note to Governor Atkins in Barbados: "You will with this packet receive a letter from his Majesty countersigned by me which, I fear, will not be very pleasing unto you, but I assure you the letter was not of my drawing but drawn by a clerk of the council in pursuance of a report made to his Majesty from the committee of plantations and by the council presented to his Majesty for his signature". On the whole, however, Charles II's Secretaries were, with the exception of Williamson, relatively little interested in colonial questions, with the result that by the end of the reign colonial governors were coming to write as a matter of course only to the lords of trade and plantations. Not until after the Board of Trade was created in 1696 did the Secretaries really join colonial battle.

The King's Servant

Patronage remained for much of the period the lubricant that kept troubled Secretaries going. The proffered gift of £4,000 to Winwood in 1614 from the pinmakers merely recognised how indispensable the Secretary continued to be as an intermediary in the securing of a monopoly from the king. But appearances were as deceptive as they had been in the sixteenth century: patronage was usually exercised on a much smaller scale than the offer to Winwood suggests; the sum expended on intelligence continued to outweigh the pitiable allowance granted for the purpose; and the burden of subsidising the personally dependent element of the secretariat became steadily more onerous. As a result Secretaries in the 1620s were bringing in over £5,000 a year gross, but at the most no more than £2,000 net. Naunton, Conway, and Dorchester all bequeathed to their descendants notably small and debt-ridden estates in consequence of their years spent in the office. Things did not really begin to look up until Thurloe, who not only received a somewhat more realistic allowance for intelligence, but also kept a masterly grip on the channels of patronage. In 1655, indeed, he was subjected to a shrewdly-directed jibe from Broghill, president of the Scottish council, after he had given a position in Scotland to a somewhat feeble in-law by the name of Lidcott. Broghill wrote to the Secretary: "For my respects to Col. Lidcott upon your command, you give me expressions which more relish of Whitehall 15 years past, than now; but in earnest, sir, I shall faithfully endeavour to serve him upon your account, as much as any man's". The criticism probably did not worry the pragmatic Thurloe, for it was hardly relevant until such time as Secretaries could afford the possibility of disinterested administration. To some extent this did become at least feasible following the Restoration, when the Secretaries began to receive quarterly grants from first the farm of the post office and later the customs that amounted to £1,850 a year for each of them. There remained in addition to this innovation four other sources of income: the formal salary of £100 a year; the allowance for intelligence, by 1675 up to £3,000 a year for the senior Secretary and £2,000 for his junior colleague; the daily board wages (i.e. in place of the actual household meals) of 16s and 6s 8d respectively; and the various fees, obtained through both formal signet warrants and the securing of direct grants from the king himself. Added to the £1,850 a year it at last represented a reasonable working income. Sunderland's agents had still to pick and choose carefully before they submitted intelligence for which they could feel relatively sure of getting reimbursed; but as far as patronage was concerned, it was now to be the developing nature of politics as much as the functional necessities of the actual office which ensured the continuing of that secretarial art once aptly described by Petre as "fishing for men in the tempestuous seas of this world".

It is hard to gauge to what extent the introduction of the annual grant of £1,850 represented a conscious acceptance of the secretaryship's public character. Certainly it was a significant revelation when in 1682 the ambassador in France wrote to the clerk of the council requesting him to pass on an enclosed communication "with as much secrecy as you can, to the king, and to choose your time when neither of the Secretaries are by", since "it relateth to his Majesty's own affairs". Moreover, the example of the contemporary French *secrétaires d' état*, recognisably modern centralising ministers, undoubtedly inspired in ambitious Francophiles like Arlington and Sunderland the desire to emulate their achievement. Yet the continental experiment of the post-Restoration era, culminating in the 1680s and the reign of James II, was for all its apparent novelty not so much modern and public in its constitutional foundations as old-fashioned and private, with the Secretary enjoying a late Indian Summer as the instrument of the king's arbitrary will. This was particularly so in the case of Sunderland, who late in 1685 showed how retrogressive his thinking was when he assumed the exalted but in practice hollow position of lord president in addition to the secretaryship. The palpable insecurity of this Secretary as he tried to implement personal rule, in however systematic a way, was reminiscent of nothing so much as Thomas Cromwell trying to cushion himself with promotions a hundred and fifty years earlier. In a sense, though, Sunderland was only reflecting the trammelled rise of the secretaryship during the seventeenth century as a whole. Thurloe during the Protectorate owed much of his pre-eminence to the putting in commission of both chancery and treasury. And in 1667 and 1668 successive orders in council ruled that any secretarial warrant involving non-secretarial expenditure must pass through the lords of the treasury before being issued. Arlington's chagrin in the early 1670s at not becoming lord treasurer himself merely anticipated the domination that Danby was to enjoy later in the decade as holder of the office. Indeed, the administrative legacy left by the 1680s was not to be Sunderland's secretaryship but rather the treasury revolution inaugurated by Godolphin, once a Secretary himself, but for four months only. Such an achievement was anyway not exactly what James II was looking for from the leading executive agent of the immediate kingly purpose.

Throughout the century it is this intimate royal connection that one is aware of again and again. "My Secretary is not in the habit of acting in matters of importance without my directions" was how James I bluntly responded to Gondomar's grievance that Naunton was victimising the Catholics in England. It was on the whole a justified boast: one has only to examine the papers of the early 1620s to see the way in which the Secretaries kept the king closely informed of almost everything that came to their attention. Things in this respect changed little under Charles I, for even an independent spirit like Falkland was

only reiterating a secretarial orthodoxy when he rebuked Prince
Rupert with the words "in neglecting me, you neglect the king". A
quarter of a century later Charles II showed how a monarch could still
regard the secretaryship in an almost medieval way when in May 1669
he wrote to his sister about Arlington that "I will be answerable for
him in what he owes you" and added some weeks later: "If I should be
deceived in the opinion I have of him, I am sure I should smart for it
most". Arlington himself was too able to be simply a pawn, but at the
same time he always remembered who ultimately was master. In 1672,
for instance, he adjusted readily to the Declaration of Indulgence and
described it to a friend as "a late deal his Majesty hath made in favour
of the Nonconformists". Coventry likewise toed the line and, in
Burnet's words, "thought himself bound to excuse if not to justify" the
king when Charles "followed the ill advices which others gave". Not
surprisingly, in view of this magisterial role, Charles himself often held
an only partially flattering opinion of his Secretaries. In 1668, indeed,
a few months before appointing Trevor, he wrote to his sister about the
would-be Secretary in a tone which suggests that the notion of raising a
man from the dust into a compliant lackey still lingered: "I am
extremely troubled that Trevor carried himself so like an ass to you. I
have sent him a chiding for it. I can say nothing for him, but that it
was a fault for want of good breeding". The necessary counterpart to
this subservience was obvious: woe betide the royal servant who
betrayed his master. Yet in 1680 Sunderland did precisely that —
"which", that astute observer Temple later commented, "for a person
actually in his service, and in such a post as Secretary of State, seemed
something extraordinary". Extraordinary, yes, and if Sunderland in
his second secretaryship was to find himself in a comparable situation
to Thomas Cromwell, then it was not inappropriate, for the consequences of his suicidal first secretaryship had shown how little the
basis of the secretarial position had changed since the similar fall of
Stephen Gardiner.

It is in this light, the perennial nexus of king and Secretary, that one
must view the symbolic importance attached during the seventeenth
century to the signet seal. With its functional use ever on the wane, it
might have been expected that the Secretary would no longer even
need to have the signet in his personal keeping. Robert Cecil in his last

years did drop the responsibility, being burdened by so many other more important ones, and a variety of royal favourites instead looked after the seal. So the pattern might have been established if James had appointed Bacon to succeed Cecil and thus followed Elizabeth's policy of utilising the secretaryship as a major ministerial office. But James after his own brief foray in the position preferred Secretaries who would act almost solely as the personal agents of his wishes; and as a result the signet necessarily returned to the secretarial keeping. In the 1620s, indeed, the Commons felt impelled to warn off Charles I from turning the clock back three hundred years and using the signet and its office as a means of getting through measures of general concern without the possible interference of either the privy seal or the great seal. Charles reluctantly took the point following a parliamentary search of the signet office for, in the words of the delegation, "such indulgences as had been granted to the papists". But the stigma remained and revealed itself with especial pertinence during the Interregnum, when the mixed fortunes of the signet seal acted as a clear guide to the various changes of political climate. Early on and again in 1659 it was discarded on account of its unconstitutional connotations; but during the Protectorate, under the auspices of Thurloe, it and the signet office were gradually reinstated and allowed to return to their old, essentially ceremonial condition. Thurloe's role in this was predictable and a measure of his ultimate conservatism as Secretary. He longed for Oliver Cromwell to assume the kingship and wrote to Henry Cromwell in July 1658 that "I have long wished that his Highness would proceed according to his own satisfaction, and not so much consider others". The lament was a reminder not only that the Secretary needed his master as much as the other way round, but also that in some underlying sense their relationship had to be exclusive as well as symbiotic if it was to flourish. The retention of the signet by the Secretaries following the Restoration served as continuing symbolic testimony to that union.

Perhaps nowhere more than in Parliament did the seventeenth-century Secretary reveal that his fundamental imperative remained that of the royal servant. Although Winwood in his inexperience boldly announced to the Commons in 1614 that he spoke there "as a Secretary of State not for the private of the king but for the public of the commonwealth", secretarial practice over the next thirty or so years belied his words. The Commons themselves had no doubts about the matter. When Calvert in December 1621 tried to explain away the arrests of Sandys as a non-parliamentary episode, the official recorder of his statement simply added "the house will scarce believe Mr. Secretary, but thinketh he equivocateth". Coke's troubled attempts later in the decade to impose the royal prerogative only hardened this sense of conflict. Matters came to a head during Windebank's last days in London. In Glyn's solemn words of accusation: "For a minister either verbally or by warrant under his own head not only to discharge men condemned but to command no further prosecution, the committee doth conceive he doth not discharge his duty". But as Windebank's private secretary, Reade, countered, his master had "done nothing but by his Majesty's order or in necessary consequence thereof". It was a reasonable defence, though unavailing at the time, and indeed sound in the context of the century as a whole. Coventry in the 1670s may have had the force and integrity of character to be on occasions the leader of the Commons as well as simply the royal protagonist there, rather like William Cecil a century earlier, but in general the secretarial role in Charles II's reign remained traditional. "Like the cherubin with his flaming sword turning it every way to defend his master's cause" was how one observer rather flamboyantly described Coventry in action. It was often an extremely wearing task, especially if the royal demands were high, as Middleton discovered on behalf of James II during the intensive six-week session of 1685. Lord Moray reported to a friend in June: "I have not had three minutes time to speak with E. Middleton this week past, he is still taken up attending the House of Commons, and tells me he can not get time to eat or sleep". As Middleton clearly realised, this was one secretarial duty for which there could be no alternative to personal involvement.

Yet the fact remains that the critical paradox in the history of the secretaryship was at its most acute during the seventeenth century. Certainly the office was still dependent upon the Crown and as a result was often filled by somewhat mediocre figures; but at the same time its responsibilities continued to broaden and deepen to an extent that eventually confirmed its status as a major ministerial position. The chequered development of the secretariat over the same period reflects perhaps more clearly than anything this transitional condition. Personal connection remained the dominant motif. "A stranger to his own business" was how in 1639 Norgate, a clerk of the signet, bitterly described his situation in a letter to Reade complaining that Coke almost exclusively used his personal clerks even for signet matters. In the other office, meanwhile, Windebank was packing the place with his own needy relatives. It was not altogether surprising therefore, given this background, that when it came to standing up and being counted in the early 1640s the staffs of the central secretariat gave meagre support to the royalist cause and chose instead to wait on events. Later in the century, however, there did begin to be apparent certain signs of loyalty to the secretariat as a department of government rather than purely to the individual Secretary as a patron. An important step came in 1675 with the payment of grants to the two chief clerks in each office; and before long the term "under-secretary" for these men had entered official usage. The obvious inspiring example was Williamson, who under Arlington had been perhaps the first chief clerk to be able to guarantee the smooth running of the office even in the Secretary's absence. And when Middleton assumed the secretaryship in 1684 he found as his chief clerk John Coke, a veteran from the days of Morrice and deputed accordingly "to judge of the style and forms of the office when anything occurs that is difficult or without precedent". Nevertheless, such men were still exceptions, since each new Secretary continued to arrive with a body of personal followers eager to fill the secretariat and take the perquisites. Charles II was only recognising a political fact when in January 1681, determined that Sunderland's influence should not linger, he dismissed as well as Sunderland himself his under-secretary William Bridgeman, even though Bridgeman had as it happened served under other Secretaries apart from Sunderland. In a turn-coat situation the fear remained and few contemporaries can have blamed Charles for not taking a gamble on the under-secretary's continuing fidelity to one of the government's most important executive departments.

The Personal Touch

The administrative and constitutional complexities of the period are such that it is possible to overlook the one basic fact of life for almost all seventeenth-century Secretaries: toil. Naunton by 1620 was complaining that he had not had a day to himself for two years. Nicholas in 1640 became clerk to the council of war because Windebank, following the dismissal of Coke, had not the time to act as its secretary. And in 1681 Daniel Finch, at the time first commissioner of the admiralty board, turned down the offer to succeed Sunderland because he knew the office would be incompatible with his family commitments. Yet to the earl of Chesterfield in August 1684 it seemed that the politicising of the major offices was rendering null the traditional governmental virtues. He wrote sarcastically with reference to the ministerial changes of that month: "I cannot but congratulate the felicity of this age, that affords so many persons equally fit for the treasury, Secretaries of State, presidents of the council, or what you please. Formerly 'twas thought these required different talents, studies and education". Even before this, indeed, Morrice in November 1667 had responded with characteristic sturdiness, in a dispatch to Winchelsea, to the interminable politicking then taking place in connection with the fall of Clarendon: "Time will bring forth and manifest the truth and instruct us by the event, but I doubt it will take up much time, the work we have cut out being not likely to be soon made up". Again, however, one can exaggerate. The secretaryship did most definitely become more political after the Restoration and especially in the eighteenth century, but it never became entirely true that the office made the man rather than the other way round. As in the Tudor period the essential secretarial qualities remained those of dedication, common-sense, and flexibility. No one in the seventeenth century epitomised them more than did Thurloe, perhaps because in the absence of an actual and therefore fallible monarch he was able to observe more scrupulously than anyone the soundest techniques of the office. Typical was an affirmation to Henry Cromwell in July 1658 about the need for a more tolerant policy towards the royalists: "We must not fix upon men only of my opinion, or of our particular way, but make it comprehensive of all the saints". Such absorptive pragmatism was indeed timeless secretarial wisdom, if only rarely emulated thereafter.

Robert Harley. By Sir Godfrey Kneller, 1714.   *National Portrait Gallery*

Henry, viscount Bolingbroke. Attributed to Alexis Simon Belle, 1712 (?)

National Portrait Gallery

William, earl of Harrington. By James Worsdale, 1746-50.
National Portrait Gallery

Thomas, duke of Newcastle. By William Hoare, c. 1752.
National Portrait Gallery

April 1757. Pitt, on the left, is distressed because of the bad state of the kingdom, but at ease with himself because his mind is honest. Fox by contrast is burdened by the knowledge of his own vices and misgovernment. On the table by him is a letter referring to the Parliamentary inquiry into the conduct of the Newcastle administration to which Fox had belonged

By permission of the Trustees of the British Museum

William Pitt, from the studio of William Hoare, c. 1754.

315

much so, to find a letter on so grave a subject, wrote without permission from hence, and afterwards suppress'd here and conceal'd from Those, who have the best right from their office to receive the earliest notice of all Incidents of this Importance, and of sea a very dangerous nature. I acknowledge my unfitness for the high station where His Majesty has been pleased to place me, but while the King

Pitt complaining to Newcastle, 1759.

George, earl of Halifax, with his two Under-Secretaries, Edward Sedgwick and Lovel Stanhope. Attributed to Daniel Gardner, after Hugh Douglas Hamilton, 1765.

National Portrait Gallery

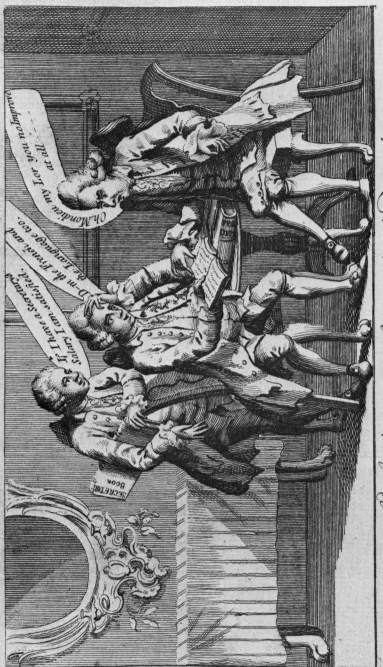

L⸺, S⸺k and his Secretary learning French.

CHAPTER FIVE

SECRETARIES OF STATE: 1689-1782

South

1689 (14th February): Charles, Duke of Shrewsbury
1690 (2nd June): Daniel, Earl of Nottingham (dismissed November 1693)

1694 (4th March): Sir John Trenchard
1695 (27th April): Charles, Duke of Shrewsbury (resigned December 1698)

1699 (14th May): Edward, Earl of Jersey (dismissed June 1700)
1700 (5th November): James Vernon

1702 (4th January): Charles, Earl of Manchester
1702 (2nd May): Daniel, Earl of Nottingham
1704 (May): Sir Charles Hedges
1706 (3rd December): Charles, Earl of Sunderland

1710 (15th June): William, Lord Dartmouth
1713 (August): Henry, Viscount Bolingbroke (dismissed August 1714)

1714 (27th September): James Stanhope
1716 (December): Paul Methuen
1717 (16th April): Joseph Addison

North

1689 (5th March): Daniel, Earl of Nottingham
1690 (26th December): Henry, Viscount Sidney (resigned March 1692)
1693 (23rd March): Sir John Trenchard
1694 (4th March): Charles, Duke of Shrewsbury
1695 (3rd May): Sir William Trumbull

1697 (2nd December): James Vernon

1700 (5th November): Sir Charles Hedges (Dismissed December 1701)
1702 (4th January): James Vernon
1702 (2nd May): Sir Charles Hedges
1704, (18th May): Robert Harley

1708 (13th February): Henry Boyle
1710 (21st September): Henry St John
1713 (17th August): William Bromley

1714 (17th September): Charles, Viscount Townshend
1716 (12th December): James Stanhope
1717 (15th April): Charles, Earl of Sunderland
1718 (March): James, Viscount Stanhope

1718 (16th March): James Craggs (died February 1721)
1721 (4th March): John, Lord Carteret

1724 (6th April): Thomas, Duke of Newcastle

1746 (10th February): John, Earl Granville: Sole Secretary until 14th February 1746
1746 (14th February): Thomas, Duke of Newcastle

1748 (February): John, Duke of Bedford
1751 (18th June): Robert, Earl of Holdernesse
1754 (23rd March): Sir Thomas Robinson (resigned October 1755)
1755 (14th November): Henry Fox (resigned November 1756)
1756 (4th December): William Pitt (dismissed 6th April 1757, reappointed 27th June 1757)
1761 (9th October): Charles, Earl of Egremont (died August 1763)

1763 (September): George, Earl of Halifax
1765 (10th July): Henry Seymour Conway
1766 (23rd May): Charles, Duke of Richmond
1766 (30th July): William, Earl of Shelburne
1768 (October): Thomas, Viscount Weymouth

1770 (December): William, Earl of Rochford

1721 (10th February): Charles, Viscount Townshend (resigned May 1730)

1730 (19th June): William, Lord Harrington
1742 (12th February): John, Lord Carteret
1744 (24th November): William, Earl of Harrington
14th February 1746
1746 (14th February): William, Earl of Harrington
1746 (29th October): Philip, Earl of Chesterfield
1748 (February): Thomas, Duke of Newcastle

1754 (March): Robert, Earl of Holdernesse (resigned 9th June 1757, reappointed 29th June 1757)

1761 (25th March): John, Earl of Bute

1762 (27th May): George Grenville
1762 (14th October): George, Earl of Halifax
1763 (9th September): John, Earl of Sandwich
1765 (10th July): Augustus, Duke of Grafton
1766 (May): Henry Seymour Conway

1768 (20th January): Thomas, Viscount Weymouth
1768 (21st October): William, Earl of Rochford
1770 (19th December): John, Earl of Sandwich

1771 (22nd January): George, Earl of Halifax
1771 (12th June): Henry, Earl of Suffolk (died March 1779)

1779 (27th October): David, Viscount Stormont (resigned March 1782)

1775 (9th November): Thomas, Viscount Weymouth
1779 (24th November): Wills, Earl of Hillsborough (resigned March 1782)

Scottish Department

1709 (3rd February): James, Duke of Queensberry (died July 1711)
1713 (30th September): John, Earl of Mar
1714 (24th September): James, Duke of Montrose (dismissed August 1715)
1716 (13th December): John, Duke of Roxburgh (dismissed August 1725)
1742 (16th February): John, Marquis of Tweeddale (resigned January 1746)

Colonial Department

1768 (20th January): Wills, Earl of Hillsborough
1772 (14th August): William, Earl of Dartmouth
1775 (10th November): Lord George Germain
1782 (17th February): Welbore Ellis (resigned March 1782)

The Secretary as Politician: 1689-1782
I. narrative

"Mr. Secretary met us and took a turn or two, and then stole away, and we both believed it was to pick up some wench; and tomorrow he will be at the cabinet with the queen: so goes the world".

D EAN Swift's memorable account of running into Henry St John in the Mall one night while taking a stroll with a friend is a reminder of the relative casualness with which Secretaries of State in the eighteenth century were able to regard the monarch. But the emphasis must be on the word "relative". Anne may have been a feeble wartime queen without a strong husband by her side and the first two Georges may have been primarily concerned about the fortunes of their Electorate of Hanover, yet access to the royal ear remained the overriding secretarial preoccupation almost as much as ever before. This is not to deny that the Secretaries had also become party politicians and ministers responsible to Parliament. As Halifax wrote to a friend in 1694 about the strong-minded King William III: "Formerly after a man had discharged a commission in foreign parts he was called home and made a Secretary of State, but that matter is a good deal altered. This King is so much a master of all foreign transactions that his choice is directed by some considerations at home more than by their skill in business abroad". A king might still, in other words, run foreign policy if he was so minded and use his

Secretaries as personal agents if it suited him; but at the same time, and these were the domestic "considerations", he needed their political support if his ministry of the day was to continue to get its way in Parliament. The result was a nice balance: on the one hand a restricted choice on the part of the Crown in finding candidates for the secretaryship; and on the other the Secretaries themselves continuing while in office to be in an old-fashioned state of dependence on the particular monarch. Such in this respect were the main consequences of the constitutional settlement of 1689. Roles and responsibilities changed somewhat, but the underlying motifs of secretarial life were still recognisable.

William III's Secretaries: 1689-1702

William III's first Secretary of State was Charles, duke of Shrewsbury, whom he appointed on 14th February 1689 after the seals had been in commission for several weeks while the revolutionary settlement was determined. Shrewsbury was a romantic figure and was once described by Swift as "the favourite of the nation", but he also tended to vacillate and lacked a certain stoicism. His politics were moderate Whiggish and he had been one of the seven prominent public men who in June 1688 invited Prince William of Orange to come to England. He is also said to have done his best on 18th December to comfort King James as the unfortunate monarch finally embarked for France. Now in 1689 he was a shade lucky to get the secretaryship: Halifax had turned the position down and William was unsure whether Shrewsbury, aged twenty-nine, had quite the experience. Nor did it in fact turn out to be a particularly happy appointment. Shrewsbury got on poorly with his fellow-Secretary, Daniel, earl of Nottingham (formerly Daniel Finch), a Tory appointed by William in March 1689 to the northern department as a deliberate balancing ploy. But their factional squabbling over appointments was as nothing compared to Shrewsbury's decision in December 1689 not to draw up William's prorogation speech for him, on the grounds that the king was too dependent for his support on untrustworthy Tories, potential Jacobites to a man. Moreover, as most of William's Secretaries found, the lack of control he was allowed to exercise over foreign affairs meant that his personal enthusiasm for the job waned quickly. Early on Shrewsbury had been diligent enough, especially in response to James's landing in Ireland in March 1689, but he became increasingly ill during the following winter, handicapped anyway by only having the use of one eye, and finally in June 1690 he resigned. "Men must live for themselves" he had written a few months earlier in a memorandum never in fact sent. And: "The toil and torture of so much business is a good bargain to none but those who are fond either of ambition, experience or money". Yet a few years later he was back, even more self-pitying than before.

Nottingham was of a quite different calibre. His temperament was somewhat stubborn, but he was also a conscientious and upright man who, though disliking the constitutional settlement reached early in 1689, subsequently upheld it loyally. Burnet did not like Nottingham, describing him as "dark, thin, and solemn", but he nevertheless wrote in the first draft of his *History of My Own Times* that in the early months of William's reign "Nottingham's being in the ministry, together with the effects that it had, first preserved the Church and then the Crown". It was an accurate tribute, yet for Nottingham himself, who in 1689 had inclined towards becoming a lord of the treasury, the role of being William's Tory Secretary was rarely other than invidious. To compensate for his lack of foreign responsibilities, for which he was in any case little qualified, he turned to naval matters, but thereby came under constant Whig attacks in the Commons. The Whigs lent their support to Admiral Russell, who by the mid-summer of 1692, after the successful battle of La Hogue, was in disagreement with Nottingham's plan to follow the victory with a naval descent on France. The dénouement came the following year. The Whigs were gaining in strength all the time in the Commons, but Nottingham in January 1693 had Russell replaced by admirals loyal to himself and later in the year paid the political price when the French took apart the English fleet destined for the Straits. In several ways the blame attached to Nottingham was unfair: he had consistently demanded that the fleet should leave at once; he had managed to locate adequate information about the movements of the French; and his colleague Trenchard, since becoming Secretary in March 1693, was in fact formally responsible for naval matters. But all this availed Nottingham little as Sunderland, back in the fray and notably unsympathetic to the secretarial plight, skilfully incited the Whigs to claim the Tory head. When William in November reluctantly demanded that the Secretary give up his seals, Nottingham's response was characteristic. He declined to return them to the king via his fellow-Secretary, as was the normal practice, and instead sent Trenchard on his way with the remark "he received 'em from his hands and so would render 'em". Later in the day he duly attended on William, who stressed that he was "entirely satisfied of his fidelity and zeal to his service". Nottingham's honour, if nothing else, was satisfied.

Shrewsbury's eventual successor as Secretary was Henry, viscount Sidney, who went to the northern department in December 1690. He was a long-standing favourite of William with a capacity for drink, intrigue, and indolence. Earlier in the year he had accompanied the king to Ireland and picked up, after the battle of the Boyne, close on 50,000 acres in forfeited estates. He was a good-natured character, but no Secretary. Soon after the appointment William asked Danby if he had passed the new Secretary as he came into the room. "No, sir! I met nobody but my Lord Sidney" was the reply. William explained: "He is the new Secretary: he will do till I find a fit man; and he will be quite willing to resign when I find such a man". Which only left Danby to make an ironic comparison between the new Secretary's role and that of a footman keeping a seat in the theatre until his social superior arrived. Sidney duly received notice to quit in March 1692, becoming lord lieutenant of Ireland, though as it happened William kept Nottingham on for a year as sole Secretary before perforce appointing the Whig-inclined Sir John Trenchard as his colleague. It was a sensible appointment in terms of easing Nottingham's work-load, but Trenchard himself had little personal aura and in 1694 lost all credibility when his obsession with Jacobitism pushed him into "exposing" the non-existent Lancashire plot. He was also dying of consumption and by the autumn of that year was out of action. After Nottingham's dismissal he had been sole Secretary, but from March 1694 was helped out, as it seemed, by the return of Shrewsbury. Although the nominally junior Secretary, Shrewsbury swiftly took over what confidential duties were allowed to the office and before very long the old pattern of complaint and attempted resignation re-established itself. In September 1696 he had a serious hunting accident and from that point allowed his private secretary, James Vernon, to fulfil the secretarial duties of all but the most formal kind. By November 1697, kept on as nominal Secretary but not allowed to attend the king because his views were at variance with those of the dominant Junto Whigs, Shrewsbury was announcing to his colleague Trumbull that he would "never sign a paper more, nor come to town, unless forced by Parliament". Finally in December 1698, after William a few months earlier had mockingly grieved over his Secretary's ill-health and added that he did not understand how becoming lord chamberlain instead would make him worse, Shrewsbury managed for the second and last time to resign.

Sir William Trumbull had been his colleague from May 1695, following Trenchard's death, until December 1697. His background was legal, though in 1683 he had gone on the same expedition to Tangier as Pepys and had been noted by the diarist as a coward. A contemporary aptly described him as "but your obedient servant to all" and his ineffectiveness as Secretary was summed up in a note he sent to his under-secretary Ellis in June 1696: "I find myself a very unfortunate squire, for when I am in town I have nothing to do, and yet nobody will suffer me to be idle out of it". This laziness proved Trumbull's undoing in 1697. With William away negotiating at Ryswick and Shrewsbury hardly ever in town, Trumbull stupidly chose to be the squire and thereby allowed Sunderland to penetrate the Junto cover through the agency of Vernon, to whom all the routine secretarial duties effectively devolved in the absence of everybody else. Vernon, essentially a competent clerk, was a pawn in Sunderland's game and in September complained to Shrewsbury, his nominal master, that Sunderland "was looking out for little men to make them Secretaries of State, and such as were framed for a dependence on a premier minister". Though Sunderland himself subsequently failed to achieve his ambitions, the secretarial part of the plan worked perfectly. Trumbull resigned in December after it had become clear to him that in the eyes of the king, the lords justices, and the run-of-the-mill petitioners he was no longer the effective Secretary. Vernon himself was not overjoyed when he heard the news: "The thing I have so long dreaded is fallen upon me", he is reputed to have said as he prepared for what was to be almost a five-year stint full of humiliating abasements. It was a measure of Vernon's lack of fibre that on Jersey's appointment in May 1699 he allowed his new colleague to go straight to the southern department, wanting neither to be involved in the French negotiations nor to be considered the senior Secretary. What one might call the Williamson tradition of elevated clerkdom had clearly found in Vernon its most enervating example.

Of Edward, earl of Jersey, appointed after a period of five months in which Vernon had been on his own following Shrewsbury's resignation, there is little to say. He had had a fair amount of diplomatic experience, unlike most of the Secretaries of the reign, and William probably hoped that, as a relatively non-political figure, he would add administrative solidity to the non-Junto ministry. But he does not seem to have contributed much and a contemporary subsequently described him as someone who had "gone through all the great offices of the kingdom, with a very ordinary understanding". In June 1700 he was dismissed and Vernon was left isolated in an increasingly charged political situation until the appointment of Sir Charles Hedges as his colleague in November. The new Secretary was a Tory sufficiently moderate and good-natured to be scornfully dismissed by the duchess of Marlborough as someone of "no capacity, no quality nor interest". His professional background was similar to that of Trumbull and he was probably the author of a pamphlet about more efficient techniques of press-ganging seamen. Hedges gave his colleague reasonably firm support, but was dismissed in December 1701 and replaced the following month by the diplomatist Charles, earl of Manchester. Vernon thereupon reverted to the northern department, which Hedges the cautious lawyer had deliberately occupied. But it mattered little, for in March 1702 William died and a few weeks later both Secretaries were dismissed. The office would not for some time be held by another such succession of mediocrities.

Anne's Secretaries: 1702-14

The secretaryship did not wholly regain its stature under Queen Anne, largely because of the dominance of Godolphin at the treasury and Marlborough at the head of the army. Nottingham and Hedges were both appointed Secretaries on 2nd May 1702 and both fared not much better second time round. Hedges only returned to the post because Nottingham insisted on having a Tory colleague alongside him; and he does not appear to have particularly imposed himself during his four-and-a-half years in office. By 1705 he was coming under great pressure from the Whigs, who were eager to have him replaced by Charles, the new earl of Sunderland, and at last in December 1706 Anne agreed that the change should take place. Nottingham, meanwhile, was long gone. Right from the start of his second secretaryship his relations with Marlborough and Godolphin were uneasy. They both felt, with some justification, that he was more concerned with satisfying the strongly Anglican wishes of the Tory "country" element than with helping to put on a broad-based administrative front aimed at winning the War of the Spanish Succession. Whig attacks against the Secretary became increasingly fierce and in the end Godolphin virtually dropped Nottingham, who resigned in May 1704. Nottingham was at pains to stress, as he wrote to a friend at the time, that it was a resignation caused by a difference of policy rather than "fear of my enemies" or "the labours, and anxious cares, of a very troublesome office". Once again he had taken the honourable way out.

Nottingham's successor was Robert Harley, whose political role was that of the moderate Tory leader prepared to back the war. He took charge of the northern department and stayed there even when Sunderland succeeded Hedges in 1706. From then on it became the normal practice for a Secretary to remain in the department he first entered, a pattern confirmed in 1709 when there ceased in a remunerative sense to be a "senior" and a "junior" Secretary. Harley himself had special responsibility for managing the Commons and even stayed on as Speaker until the dissolution in 1705. It was a task well suited to his outlook, which preferred the process of government to the conflict of party and probably lay behind his final falling-out with Marlborough and Godolphin in February 1708. Even in December 1706 he had strongly disapproved of the appointment of Sunderland, whom he saw as a hot Whig and a trouble-maker. It was a legitimate opinion of his new colleague, who was the son of Robert, son-in-law of Marlborough, and when aged only fourteen had been described by Evelyn as "a youth of extraordinary hopes, very learned for his age, and ingenious". As Secretary he showed little respect for Queen Anne, who complained how he always "chose to reflect in a very injurious manner upon all previous Princes as a proper entertainment for her". Typically it was Sunderland who was to the fore in instigating the impeachment and subsequent trial in March 1710 of the high churchman Dr Henry Sacheverell. He received little support from Henry Boyle, his fellow-Secretary since February 1708. Boyle was a mild figure who represented the ministry faithfully in the Commons and to whom Addison dedicated the third volume of the *Spectator* with the tribute that he knew of no politician who had "made himself more friends and fewer enemies". The odium attached to the Sacheverell affair did indeed bring down the Whigs, as Boyle had feared. Queen Anne dismissed Sunderland in June 1710 — with the Secretary declining a pension on the haughty grounds that "if he could not have the honour to serve his country he would not plunder it" — and Boyle himself resigned in September. As Secretary he had been forced to act as one of the managers of the trial and wisely he decided not to stand in the elections the following month. Unlike his impetuous colleage he was not to return to the secretaryship.

The new head of the queen's ministry was Harley, who even before Godolphin fell in August 1710 had shown his influence by securing the moderate Tory, William, Lord Dartmouth, to be Sunderland's successor. The new Secretary's administrative abilities were negligible, but he suited Harley's purposes. Not surprisingly he was soon over-shadowed by Boyle's brilliant replacement, Henry St John, who between 1704 and 1708 had been secretary at war, but was still a young man. As the Austrian ambassador in London, Count Gallas, conceded in 1711: "To talk to Dartmouth is like talking to a brick-wall. St John is just the opposite. He investigates everything, takes everything in, and can always be relied upon to make a formal statement". There was of course the other well-known side to St John. In the famous words of the prostitute on hearing that he had become a minister: "Seven thousand guineas a year, my girls, and all for us!" His profligate activities, however, rarely affected either his work as Secretary or his determination to lead the Tory "country" party and oust Harley, treasurer from 1711, from his position of political domination. For almost four years the two men fought out a bitter and involved struggle, concentrating for much of the time on control over the peace negotiations with France, though early on St John ignored his ministerial responsibilities, and anticipated his state of permanent opposition after 1714, when he encouraged "country" demands for an inquiry into treasury corruption. In August 1713 Harley attempted to strengthen his hand by replacing Dartmouth with William Bromley, an honest and respected Tory who had been Speaker since 1710 and now continued to lend his support to the treasurer, but who somehow lacked the necessary inner steel to be a major force. In the end the titans knocked each other out: St John (or viscount Bolingbroke as he was from 1712) whittled away at Harley's influence through the queen's friend Lady Masham and on 27th July 1714 the treasurer fell; but at that crucial moment St John's nerve seemed to break and four days later Queen Anne herself died, the final blow to Tory hopes. The new regime was manifestly going to be Hanoverian, Protestant, and Whig. St John in panic fled the country and in July 1715 was appointed the Old Pretender's secretary of state. It proved a hollow, thankless task and St John was quite unfairly blamed for failing to get adequate supplies in time to Scotland. In March 1716 James Edward dismissed him. St John's executive duties were over and the even more unrewarding life of a Tory propagandist in Whig England stretched ahead.

Early Hanoverian Secretaries: 1714-24

The new Secretary in the southern department (to which St John had transferred in 1713 in order to get a firmer grip on the French situation) was James Stanhope, the most able diplomatist of his generation. Hitherto his main achievements had been military, culminating in 1708 in a leading role in the capture of Minorca. Indeed, his immediate response when he was offered the secretaryship was to touch his sword as a gesture to indicate where he thought his best talents lay. But eventually he was prevailed upon to accept and he soon showed himself to be a foreign minister of great perception, honesty, and sustained patriotic purpose. His colleague was Charles, viscount Townshend, who late in Anne's reign had shrewdly developed his relations with the Elector George's ministers Bothmer and Robethon and as a result became chief minister himself following the Hanoverian succession. His sincerity was patent, but for all his wide diplomatic experience in the 1700s he does not appear to have possessed the political imagination necessary to carry the position of leading minister. The two Secretaries were personal friends, Whigs by outlook, and served George I well during the Jacobite rebellion of 1715. In the aftermath neither proved exceptionally vengeful and Stanhope indeed was said to have spared Lord Nairn's life because they had been boys together at Eton. In 1716, however, ministerial unity withered away. Stanhope in July accompanied George to Hanover and in their absence Townshend naïvely moved close enough to the Prince of Wales to inspire malicious and personally damaging conspiracy rumours. He was also in disagreement with Stanhope's foreign policy, the corner-stone of which was the French alliance of November 1716, regarded by Townshend as over-hasty. The following month George dismissed him. Townshend's successor was the capable diplomatist Paul Methuen, who had been doing Stanhope's work in the southern department since July and now stayed there. Stanhope himself transferred to the northern sphere, which had by now assumed the greater importance with a German on the throne. The new combination only lasted until April 1717, when the Whigs split: Townshend resigned from his new position as lord-lieutenant of Ireland, taking with him his brother-in-law Sir Robert Walpole at the treasury and Methuen also. Stanhope kept going at the head of the ministry, but felt the political need to take over Walpole's duties and therefore reluctantly abandoned the secretaryship. He would be back soon, but not before a curious eleven months in the history of the office.

Sunderland, as untrustworthy as ever, now returned as the northern Secretary. Characteristically he got the job by speeding over to Hanover late in 1716 and giving the king a steady dose of stories directed against Townshend and Walpole. His subsequent appointment showed that he was back in political favour, though in practice Stanhope retained much of the control over foreign matters in his own hands. Sunderland's colleague was the poet and essayist Joseph Addison, who since 1714 had been acting for much of the time as Sunderland's private secretary. The appointment occasioned the predictable response: "Who would have expected to have seen the head of the poets a Secretary of State?" asked a contemporary. There were in fact many worse Secretaries than Addison. Though he did not enjoy his duties in the Commons and found the drafting of a dispatch surprisingly difficult, he was nevertheless honest and generally competent in the performance of his duties. His health was poor, however, and even less than a year as Secretary almost finished him. The night of 2nd November 1717 was particularly afflicting in this respect. Late that night he attended at Hampton Court, as a Secretary was bound to, the Princess giving birth to a son. By three in the morning he was back home in Kensington, only to receive a message from the Princess's lady-in-waiting that her mistress desired the usual stay of execution for condemned felons. This in turn necessitated getting George's permission, which was obtained by five. Addison thereupon countersigned the relevant warrants and crawled thankfully into bed. Four months later he resigned. By so doing he followed hard on the heels of Sunderland, though his object was not the comforts of retirement, but instead an attempt to control the treasury and thereby regulate political patronage.

Stanhope (now a viscount) accordingly returned to the secretaryship and his colleague in the southern department was James Craggs, son of the corrupt postmaster-general. The young Craggs was possessed of a sharp mind that enabled him on behalf of Stanhope to counter the attacks mounted on the ministry by Walpole in the Commons. It was a measure of his contemporary reputation that his predecessor Addison, in his dying days in 1719, dedicated his works to him. Stanhope meanwhile dominated foreign affairs, even to the extent of supervising the negotiations that led up to the treaty of Passarowitz in July 1718, though theoretically it was a "southern" matter. The two Secretaries got on well together and indeed, as after a long marriage, followed each other into the grave in February 1721. Rumours abounded about the cause of this sudden rash of mortality. Lord Harley wrote to his father soon afterwards: "The great debauch which killed Stanhope and Craggs was at the Duke of Newcastle's. They drank excessively of new tokay, champagne, visney, and barba water, thirteen hours it is said". The probable truth was more creditable. Although not implicated personally, Stanhope was deeply worried about the South Sea Bubble which had burst the previous year and on 4th February was seized by apoplexy while addressing the House of Lords. The following day he died and George was apparently unable to eat his supper when he heard the news. Eleven days later smallpox took the younger

Craggs. His father, involved in the Bubble as part of his ambition to store up riches for his son, survived but a month. The stage was set for Walpole to return as first lord of the treasury, chancellor of the exchequer, and all-round political master.

Even before the younger Craggs died, Townshend had returned to the northern department to replace Stanhope. With the country in an unsettled state he showed distinct strong-arm tendencies and in October 1722 authorised the temporary suspension, for over a year in the event, of *habeas corpus*. His colleague from March 1721 was John, Lord Carteret, whom Townshend kept in check by the tactic of staying as close as possible to the king's side on royal visits to Hanover. It was as well for Townshend that he did, because Carteret was a favourite of George, being possessed not only of the ability to converse in German, unlike the other members of the ministry, but also the propensity to discourse on foreign affairs in an alluringly grand manner. Unfortunately, though, he over-reached himself. By 1723 he alone was adopting a pro-Imperial stance, in contrast to the pro-French line of Walpole, Townshend, and Newcastle that had become the accepted principle in the conduct of foreign policy. Late in that year it was brought to George's attention that his Secretary was manoeuvring behind Louis XV's back in French court politics and in April 1724 Carteret was forced to resign. Walpole could have chosen Pulteney to succeed him, but instead preferred the much less talented Thomas, duke of Newcastle, partly because of the duke's substantial pocket of electoral control, but even more because, in Hervey's words, Walpole "looked upon his understanding to be such as could never let him rise into a dangerous rival". Newcastle was to be Secretary for a record period of thirty years and for almost half that time justified Walpole's expectations that he would be a deferential subordinate. But eventually the worm turned and Newcastle managed to retrieve a little of the authority of the secretaryship that the earlier part of his tenure had seriously undermined.

The Scottish Secretaryship

The Newcastle era in secretarial history was preceded, however, by the creation of a third secretaryship, with the holder of the post being specifically responsible for Scottish affairs but on a par in terms of status with the other two Secretaries of State. It enjoyed only a spasmodic existence during the eighteenth century, but pointed the way to subsequent sub-divisions of the secretaryship. The first man to assume the position was James, duke of Queensberry, appointed in February 1709, two years after the Act of Union, as the third Principal Secretary of State. Unlike his successors he was not confined to responsibility for Scottish affairs only: relations with Russia, Poland, Denmark, and Sweden were all included within his province after the fall of Sunderland, with whom Queensberry had persistently quarrelled since his appointment about their respective fees and authority. The appointment did not turn out to be a propitious one. Godolphin had introduced the idea as a way of making the Scots aware of where the official source of patronage lay, but Queensberry himself was an unscrupulous character in whose hands the position became merely one more weapon in the factional politics of the Scottish nobility. His own tendencies were Tory and probably for that reason Harley kept him on until his death in June 1711. The treasurer thereupon left the post in abeyance and, doubtless reluctantly, allowed St John in the northern department to take over the Scottish duties.

It proved a short interlude. Harley by 1713 was doing everything he could to contain St John's influence and in September, even though his rival had moved to the southern department a month earlier, he had John, earl of Mar appointed as the third Secretary. Mar lasted only a year, but in that time he was able to establish his authority over Scottish business despite early opposition from St John and Bromley. When Argyll fell from favour, it was St John who dismissed him from all his English offices, but Mar who stripped him of the governorship of Edinburgh Castle. Mar was, however, a turn-coat tainted by Jacobitism; and after Queen Anne died he found himself in as untenable a position as his two fellow-Secretaries. His successor in September 1714 was James, duke of Montrose, an over-sensitive figure who had fallen badly foul of Rob Roy Macgregor. Stanhope and Townshend reckoned him too pusillanimous to be Secretary when the Jacobite rebels under Mar actually arrived and in August 1715 he was dismissed. A gap then followed until the appointment in December 1716 of John, duke of Roxburgh, a Stanhope nominee. He was an accomplished man who had done well in 1715 at the battle of

Sheriffmuir and now lasted far longer as third Secretary than any of his predecessors. After Stanhope's death, however, Roxburgh made the understandable but serious mistake of looking to Carteret for guidance rather than Townshend and above him Walpole. By 1723 an astute observer in London saw what was in the wind: "If I guess right, Walpole's scheme is to let all the Scots act as individuals and consequently depend on those in powere here". So it proved. Roxburgh in 1725 tacitly lent his support to riots in Glasgow against the new malt tax and Walpole was thus enabled to secure from George I his dismissal. The first lord of the treasury decided against naming a successor and Scottish business was instead conducted nominally through Newcastle in the southern department, but in practice by Walpole himself through the person of Duncan Forbes, the tough-minded pro-Union lord advocate. The very fact that he did not appoint a new third Secretary of his own choosing showed how strong Walpole felt his own political position to be.

Such was the eighteenth-century history of this third secretaryship, apart from a short and unmemorable tail-piece in the 1740s. This was the tenure of John, marquis of Tweeddale, appointed in February 1742, a month after Walpole's fall. The new Secretary lacked calibre as a man of affairs and is best known rather for the high quality of the timber cultivated on his estate in East Lothian. He had only been appointed because of his consistent adherence to the men of the hour, Pulteney and Carteret, and by 1744 he was causing his fellow-Secretaries much anxiety because of his complacent attitude to the threat of another Jacobite rising. The rebellion duly happened the following year and Tweeddale's response was so feckless that in January 1746 he was virtually compelled to resign in order to ensure anti-Jacobite solidity on the part of an important group of Scottish noblemen. Newcastle reassumed responsibility for Scotland, a duty which followed him to the northern department in 1748, but once again it was the lord advocate who played a quasi-ministerial role and exercised the greater influence in the dispensation of patronage. The system worked well enough in terms of ensuring a compliant nation; and when the third secretaryship was revived in the second half of the century, its concerns lay with an altogether different and more devolutionary area of the world.

Newcastle and Pitt: 1724-60

In December 1754, shortly after giving up the secretaryship, Newcastle received a request for help from Hardwicke the lord chancellor. Hardwicke explained that two people needed to be favoured, but that only one place was vacant, and went on: "I don't pretend to know how, but your Grace, who has great dexterity in turning & shaping those things, may be able to chalk it out". It was a fair tribute to the supremely eighteenth-century techniques of man management which Newcastle had perfected during his thirty years as Secretary. One private note he made while Secretary suggests the basis of his approach to public affairs: "Thomas Newman, smuggler in Horsham Gaol; has many friends in Sussex; to be released. — 40 or 50 double votes depend on this". Nevertheless, Newcastle has perhaps been given too bad a press and, if never a first-rate statesman, did in the course of time come to be something more than just a particularly able politician. His attention to detail was usually meticulous and if he had possessed the ability to lead he would probably have been a great politician of his age. His early years as Secretary, however, could hardly have been less incisive. At the time of his appointment he had never been abroad and he wrote soon afterwards to Horace Walpole about the conduct of foreign affairs: "I shall in everything act in concert with my Lord Townshend and according to the advice & instructions that I shall have the pleasure of receiving from him". But by 1727, as Walpole began to move against Townshend, he was starting to acquire under the auspices of the first lord a rather less inhibited voice. Townshend himself was at the same time coming under criticism from the new king, George II, who delivered against him the harsh verdict of "a choleric blockhead". The inevitable break finally came in May 1730, when Townshend resigned after finding himself in a party of one about pursuing an implacably anti-Imperial policy. In disgust he retired to his lands in Norfolk and there developed the experiments with root crops that were to earn him the celebrated nickname "Turnip".

His successor was William, Lord Harrington, previously ambassador in Spain, to whom Newcastle wrote on his appointment: "God bless Sir Robert — 'tis all his doing; and let us in return, resolve to make him happy as we can". The new Secretary had deep down a stubborn streak, but on the whole it suited his temperament to tag along. The queen hated him ("there is a heavy, insipid sloth in that man that puts me out of all patience") and by 1736 Harrington's position was in such decline that even George, who liked his pro-German attitude, did not invariably take him on trips to Hanover. Newcastle meanwhile was continuing in the first half of the 1730s to bow to Walpole, even to the extent of acting as the dumb go-between in the correspondence between the first lord and Waldegrave at Versailles. In many ways it was a thankless life for both Secretaries and they probably only clung on in office because they needed a guaranteed salary to stave off creditors. In the second half of the decade, however, Newcastle at least began to fight back. Partly he did so by encroaching increasingly on his fellow-Secretary's authority; partly by becoming a more assertive figure in colonial matters; but above all by forcing Walpole in October 1739 to accept rising public opinion and declare war against Spain. As it turned out Newcastle did not distinguish himself as a wartime Secretary. Typical was a panicky note to Hardwicke: "For God's sake, my dear Lord, let us put our fleets upon action, somewhere, or all will be called a farce". And on another occasion: "You ask me, why does not Sir Chaloner Ogle sail? I answer, because he is not ready. If you ask another question, why is he not ready? to that I cannot answer". In the end, though, it was Walpole and with him Harrington whom the war brought down, not Newcastle. Much of the old guard remained to support the duke; and Carteret, for so long out of office, knew that he was in for a difficult time when in February 1742 he initiated his ministry and personally assumed the secretaryship for the north.

Newcastle and Carteret were not long falling out, though in the early stages both made a conscious effort to get on together. The blame was probably about equal. Carteret was determined to keep all significant foreign business in his own hands; while Newcastle, ever more worried about his colleague's close relations with the king, began to repudiate Carteret's lukwarmness towards Austria as being more in the Hanoverian than the English interest. By the end of 1743 the two Secretaries would not even eat at the same table and the following year Newcastle, helped by Carteret's own failings as a war minister, was able to bring him down. Harrington returned as Secretary, as before under Newcastle's sway, and held the position until October 1746, apart from four absurd days in February earlier that year. This brief hiatus was occasioned by the resignation of the entire ministry under Pelham (Newcastle's brother) in response to the lack of royal confidence the ministers were receiving. Newcastle characteristically pushed Harrington in before him during the actual submission of the seals of office, with the result that by the time he came to resign the king was getting used to the idea, whereas George never forgave Harrington for what he regarded as his perfidy. Sole Secretary for the next four days, and unable to form a cohesive ministry, was Granville, formerly Carteret. Soon afterwards he described the experience: "I was sitting quietly by my fireside, reading in my study; the King sends to me to take the seals. I saw 'twould not do and was amazed at it. But like a dutiful subject of the Crown I obeyed. I waited on the King. I took the seals, went directly to my office, wrote a few letters of form, and signed a pass. That's all the business I have done". Or as he observed at the time when asked why he had not communicated his appointment to the envoy at Florence: "To Italy? No, before the courier can get there I shall be out again". George meanwhile was grasping the point of the farce and speedily recalled the Pelham ministry. The unlucky Harrington, however, was soon to be pushed into a final resignation. He felt that he had no alternative after discovering, while peace negotiations were going on at Breda, that Newcastle had been corresponding behind his back even more than usual. The tactic was deliberate and over the next eight years became a familiar gambit as Newcastle, in his last phase as Secretary, behaved not unlike a rich widow ruthlessly working her way through a succession of unsatisfactory consorts.

His first colleague after Harrington was Philip, earl of Chesterfield, best remembered for being the cause of Dr Johnson's substituting "the patron" for "the garret" as one of the five ills of the scholar's life. Now in October 1746, with his good intellect and recent experience as lord lieutenant of Ireland, he was confident that he could handle the situation. He was soon writing to an ambassador in his province with the tone of someone big enough to absorb a pettily ambitious colleague: "Pray continue to write separate letters to the Duke of Newcastle, if you would continue to be well with him; for he is a jealous lover of paper". They were well-turned words, but Chesterfield's secretaryship showed him crucially lacking in political resolution. He allowed himself to be dominated by Newcastle and by the end of 1747 was complaining, according to Hardwicke, that "he had *beaucoup à faire, rien à dire*". Soon afterwards, in February 1748, he swallowed his pride and resigned. His successor was John, duke of Bedford, who had previously held an admiralty post and about whom Richmond wrote acutely to Newcastle: "My only objection against your new colleague is that if you do not agree together, you can not get rid of him so easily as of the last". So indeed it turned out, though Newcastle at the outset took the precaution of transferring to the northern department so that he could cover German matters and thereby stay close to the king. Bedford as Secretary was not only incorrigibly idle, spending most of his time at Woburn, but also spoke persistently in opposition to Newcastle's unimaginative foreign policy of subsidising all possible continental allies. In June 1751, however, Newcastle successfully incited him to resign by first securing the dismissal of John, earl of Sandwich, Bedford's young follower at the admiralty and a former protégé of Newcastle himself. It was from Newcastle's point of view a happy moment, for in Bedford's successor he finally found a faithful retainer. Robert, earl of Holdernesse had in his youth been very keen on staging operas and on his appointment to the secretaryship the following epigram circulated:

"That secrecy will not prevail
    In politics is certain;
Since Holdernesse, who gets the seals,
    Was bred behind the curtain".

In fact Holdernesse as Secretary kept his mouth closed and amply justified the praised bestowed upon him by Newcastle at the time of his appointment that "he has no pride about him, though a D'Arcy". Holdernesse's political and administrative abilities were negligible, but such was precisely his attraction. Apart from a three-week gap in 1757 he stayed as Secretary for close on ten years and seems never to have risen in the general esteem. "That formal piece of dullness", Horace Walpole called him, and unfortunately the evidence does not point to the contrary.

At last, in March 1754, Newcastle gave up the secretaryship, following the death of Pelham. He succeeded his brother as first lord of the treasury, but not perforce as leader of the Commons, which duty he delegated to Sir Thomas Robinson, the incoming Secretary. It proved a disastrous move. "The Duke might as well have sent his jack boot to lead us", remarked William Pitt, the rising political force of the day. Robinson was a Walpole man who had spent much of his life as ambassador in Vienna and only accepted the secretaryship unwillingly. His character was pompous and pedantic and in November 1755, after a relentless battering from Pitt, he was thankful to give way to Henry Fox, who had in fact already taken over Robinson's parliamentary duties a few weeks earlier. Newcastle now exploited his new Secretary with a similar selfishness. "The King will not suffer Mr. Fox to do anything, even in the House of Commons, without consulting me", he observed complacently to his sister-in-law soon afterwards. Yet Fox had done Newcastle a considerable favour by replacing Robinson, after actually refusing the secretaryship in March 1754, and was with his agile mind and impressive countenance the only man apart from Pitt capable of giving the ministry credibility in the Commons. During 1756, as a major conflict between the European powers became more and more inevitable, Newcastle allowed the situation to fall apart completely. Early in the year Fox was noting: "All agree a war is unavoidable, but Ld Chancellor and the D. of Newcastle are for a little paper war first, for which I shall, I doubt not, receive orders this forenoon". And Pitt in May described Newcastle as like "a child in a go-cart upon the brink of a precipice". Matters came to a head in the autumn with the country at war and Minorca surrendered. Fox, who could take no more of Newcastle's duplicity, abandoned his duties; and Pitt in December assumed the secretaryship on the condition that Newcastle left office. "I know that I can save this country, and that no one else can", he affirmed with the confidence of a believer and gradually others came to believe it also.

Pitt's tenure of the office for the greater part of the Seven Years War was without doubt the most notable phase in secretarial history since the sixteenth century. "The Great Commoner" contemporaries called him and it suggested very well the man's pugnacious spirit in an age when privilege and self-satisfied ineptitude seemed to go hand in hand. From an early age he had hated Walpole and everything his rule had epitomised. Not surprisingly, George II in 1756 viewed his

Secretary with considerable suspicion and in April the following year dismissed him. But there could be no alternative to Pitt until the war had been won and in June the king brought him back, along with Holdernesse, who had resigned three weeks earlier in what turned out to be a successful ploy to have Newcastle reinstated at the treasury. The episode taught Pitt as well as George a lesson. Pitt now perceived not only that it would be folly to ignore Hanoverian considerations entirely as he planned the war, but also that he must allow Newcastle to deploy his well-seasoned control over patronage if he himself as Secretary was to have a united political nation behind him. Such was the necessary basis on which Pitt now proceeded to become one of England's greatest war ministers. The zenith was reached in 1759, when Horace Walpole declared not altogether extravagantly that "our bells are worn threadbare with ringing for victories". Perhaps Pitt's most valuable quality in these years was his ability to inspire passion and conviction in other men's hearts. In January 1758, after an eloquent oration to the Commons had secured £100,000 for the allied cause, a Polish prince who had been present remarked that it was less the speech of a Secretary of State than of a tribune of the people. So it doubtless was, but therein lay Pitt's singular powers of motivation. At the same time, moreover, he stood firmly in the sixteenth-century secretarial tradition of unsparing attention to detail. His seasonal pattern was to spend the winter months elaborating the strategy for the forthcoming campaigns and then within that framework to allow his commanders in the field the initiative during the actual fighting, while all the time maintaining a close watch from London. Typical of his approach was this passage from an extremely long dispatch which he sent in December 1757 to General Abercromby in America: "It is the King's pleasure, that you do take particular care to send, in due time, the said entire battering train, together with the stores above-mentioned, to Halifax, in order that the same may be in readiness to be employed for the siege of Louisbourg, intended to be undertaken as early as is pointed out in the foregoing part of this letter". Granted the almost insuperable difficulties of communication, it proved probably the best method, allowing Pitt to impose his political acumen and wide-ranging strategical perspective on the specific military situation. George II among others came round in time to appreciating the

indispensability of his Secretary. But in October 1760 the king died
and was succeeded by George III, determined to reverse everything he
believed his grandfather had stood for. Within weeks Pitt was
complaining that "I and my Lord Holdernesse dangle at court with a
bag in our hands, but we are not ministers". An era of favourites was
returning for the last time and with it the end of a short but
remarkable secretaryship.

George III's Secretaries: 1760-82

To try to account for the political instability of the first ten years of
George III's reign is a complex task, inextricably linked with the new
king's stubborn attempt to establish a personal rule, but suffice to say
that the instability existed and had the effect of producing a be-
wilderingly rapid turn-over of Secretaries. The first to go was
Holdernesse, replaced in March 1761 by John, earl of Bute, the
pro-peace Scottish nobleman in whom George reposed an almost
child-like trust. Early on he made a dead set against Pitt and in
October, amidst much popular hostility, had his way. "I will be
responsible for nothing that I do not direct", Pitt enunciated to the
cabinet three days before his resignation. The new Secretary was
Charles, earl of Egremont, a competent and well-informed figure
who spent most of 1762 trying to prevent Bute from authorising peace
at any price with France. His ally in this cause was George Grenville,
who in April 1762 became Secretary when Bute went to the treasury.
But in October the same year Grenville lost his position when Bute
(soon himself to abandon the pressures of high office) decided that the
Secretary's heart was not in the job of getting the peace terms through
the Commons. Bute instead delegated the task to Fox, who during the
ensuing winter used the corruptest possible means to fulfil the brief,
but obstinately declined to become Secretary himself. The actual
office fell to George, earl of Halifax, a former president of the board of
trade who suffered during the 1760s from a place-hunting mistress and
now held the secretaryship until July 1765. Egremont remained as his
colleague until August 1763, when he died of apoplexy shortly after
making the memorable pronouncement: "Well, I have but three turtle
dinners to come, and if I survive them I shall be immortal". He was
replaced by Sandwich, who like Halifax stayed in the office until July

1765. During his secretaryship he played a leading role in the prosecution of John Wilkes, an old associate, and thereby earned the nickname "Jemmy Twitcher" as a mark of his unpopularity. The temporary end for both Secretaries came in 1765 with the fall of the Grenville ministry as a result of the misliked Stamp Act that attempted to deal with the question of the American colonies. Once again Pitt was ready and expectant in the wings.

First, though, the Whig leader the marquis of Rockingham had his turn in charge of a ministry. Halifax's successor in the southern department was Henry Seymour Conway, an honest man and brave soldier but no politician, though he did manage early in 1766 to get through the repeal of the Stamp Act — with, as Burke described it, "the face of an angel". The other Secretary was Augustus, duke of Grafton, appointed as a concession to Pitt and in the event leaving office in May 1766, two months before most of his colleagues, to help make way for a ministry under Pitt. Somewhat ingenuously, considering his penchant for hounds and horse-racing, he told the Lords that he was resigning not "from a love of ease and indulgence to his private amusements, as had been falsely reported, but because they wanted strength, which one man only could supply". Meanwhile, until Pitt actually formed his ministry in July, Rockingham replaced Grafton with Charles, duke of Richmond, a young soldier and diplomatist who had not nearly enough standing for the office. Finally, the much-awaited change came. Pitt surprised everyone by becoming the earl of Chatham and lord privy seal, as a result of which he decided to retain Conway (in the northern department since May) as Secretary in order to represent the ministry in the Commons. Conway found the task beyond him and by May 1767 was trying in vain to persuade George to allow him to resign, "without any view", Conway stressed like a true soldier, "of entering into faction". Secretary for the south and therefore the American colonies as well was William, earl of Shelburne, who was charged by Pitt with the job of conciliating the colonies. To do so he was instructed to assume all the responsibilities in that sphere which the intransigent board of trade had recently been marking out for itself. It was a difficult task, made trebly so by 1767 with the permanent absence of Pitt on account of illness and an almost total lack of cabinet support for Shelburne in his resistance to the contrary American policy of Townshend, the chancellor of the exchequer, whose hard-line attitude continued to influence ministerial thinking even after his early death in September that year. Conway in January 1768 at last managed to resign and in the same month a third secretaryship, with responsibility for the colonies, was created in order to implement George's policy of no surrender. Grafton meanwhile attempted to lead the ministry in Pitt's absence, but was found lacking in the strength of will necessary to impose himself. In January 1770 he resigned and to form a new ministry George turned to the plodding Lord North, appointed him first lord of the treasury, and prepared to dig in. Even more than in the early part of the reign, Secretaries were now only valuable, and indeed had been so since Pitt's decline, if they were willing to serve as the king's acquiescent tools.

It was hardly surprising, then, that the northern and southern departments were filled between 1768 and 1782 by a succession of mediocrities or political lightweights. Conway's replacement was Thomas, viscount Weymouth, far too dissolute a character to harness his oratorical abilities, but a firm figure during the rioting of 1768 occasioned by Wilkes's imprisonment. In December 1770 he resigned, possibly because he was anxious not to be still a minister if the dispute with Spain over the Falkland Islands turned into a war. Since October 1768, when Shelburne had resigned, Weymouth's colleague in the other long-established department had been William, earl of Rochford, a good-natured character with diplomatic experience, but carrying little authority. His moment of truth came in May 1769 when his was the casting vote which defeated Grafton's proposal to the cabinet that the recent fiscal duties imposed on the American colonies should be repealed. Rochford stayed as Secretary until November 1775 and probably resigned only because of being ordered to pay damages of £1,000 as a result of having one Sayn arrested, and his papers seized, on no specific charge, contrary to recent legal rulings. During his tenure of office two former Secretaries had acted in the northern department as colleagues: Sandwich between December 1770 and January 1771, whereupon he returned to the admiralty for the rest of the decade; and Halifax from January 1771 until his death in June that year. So reduced by drink and debts was Halifax in these last months that George wrote to North on his appointment: "Had I been in his situation and of his age, I should have preferred his motto, *otium cum dignitate*". Halifax's successor was Henry, earl of Suffolk, who held the secretaryship until his death in March 1779, despite being, in the words of a contemporary, "dead to the State long before he was dead to nature". Weymouth meanwhile had returned in November 1775 to replace Rochford and occupied the office until resigning four years later in consequence of his opinion that the war with America was no longer sustainable. This left the way open for the last two Secretaries of the northern and southern departments: David, viscount Stormont and Wills, earl of Hillsborough respectively. Stormont was a diplomatist of wide experience and was also said to have been the most scholarly person whom Winckelmann the historian ever met, but as Secretary of State, replacing Suffolk after a gap of almost eight months, he left no mark. Hillsborough, however, was somewhat different. His abilities were limited, but he attained prominence through his stubborn attachment to the royal point of view. As late as November 1781 he was telling the Lords how he wished that "the independence of America would never be admitted in that House". The wish was of little relevance, coming only four months before he and Stormont resigned with the rest of the North ministry, but it did have a certain historical interest coming from Hillsborough's lips. For he it was who in 1768 had been the first Secretary of State specifically responsible for the colonies; and in the colonial department lay the real centre of the secretaryship during these last fourteen years.

The Colonial Secretaryship

Hillsborough's appointment as Secretary of State for the colonies resolved the long-standing conflict between Secretaries for the south and successive presidents of the board of trade, of whom Hillsborough himself had been one from 1763 to 1765 and then from 1766 up to his secretarial appointment. There was then a short period in which Clare was president, but from July 1768 until 1779 it was always the third Secretary who assumed the position as part of his secretarial functions. The cause for which Halifax had fought so stubbornly in the 1750s as president of the board of trade had been lost. That there was an administrative need for a third secretaryship there was little doubt. Newcastle in his old age was affirming in 1766 that the work-load for the southern Secretary had become intolerable and Henry Wilmot, a colonial agent, observed shortly after the creation of the third secretaryship that if it had taken place sooner "it would have given greater dispatch and lessened expense". But Hillsborough himself was a poor choice, possessing as he did the unfailing knack of rubbing people up the wrong way. By 1771 Benjamin Franklin was not alone in feeling aggrieved by the Secretary's "perverse and senseless management". Hillsborough was also coming under pressure from his two fellow-Secretaries as part of their pin-pricking anti-North campaign and in August 1772 he resigned. His successor, after Weymouth had turned down the office on account of what he saw as its lack of proper secretarial status, was William, earl of Dartmouth. The new Secretary's political experience was limited, his administrative talents nil, and he had the nickname "the Psalmsinger" because of his evangelical leanings. Franklin had been desirous of his appointment while Hillsborough was still Secretary, but following the change he was compelled to describe Dartmouth as "a truly good man" who "wishes sincerely a good understanding with the colonies, but does not seem to have strength equal to his wishes". It was a just assessment. Suffolk still had life enough to dominate the conduct of colonial matters and once the American war had started in 1775 even George, who liked Dartmouth personally, had to admit that a change was necessary. Dartmouth accordingly resigned in November and was replaced by the more militant Lord George Germain.

The appointment surprised most people and put Horace Walpole in mind of an aphorism that Lansdowne had once coined during a period in the Tower: "Some fall so hard, they bound and rise again". Walpole was thinking of Germain's disgrace after he had three times, at the battle of Minden in 1759, refused orders to charge issued by the commander-in-chief, Prince Ferdinand, whom he cordially disliked. Germain was fortunate not to be shot, but gradually his quick turn of mind, forceful oratory, and imperious bearing won him back into royal favour. By the mid-1770s he was insisting that the American colonies were essentially a military problem and it was this approach which doubtless prompted George to appoint him Secretary. "A Roman severity" was just the right phrase to appeal to the king. As one might expect, Germain's failings as Secretary were considerable. His disposition was too moody, he lacked the long view, and above all he attempted to control far too minutely the commanding officers in the field. As Clinton pleaded to him in 1779: "For God's sake, my Lord, if you wish me to do anything, leave me to myself, and let me adapt my efforts to the hourly change of circumstances". Moreover, Germain had the pervasive secretarial habit of going behind the backs of the commanders and dealing secretly with their junior officers. In several ways, however, his reputation as Secretary is unfairly wretched. It was of course a bad war to lose, but it is difficult to hold Germain solely, or perhaps even primarily, responsible for the conduct of Burgoyne that resulted in the surrender at Saratoga in 1777. Nor subsequently did he fail to perceive the necessity of attempting to woo the Loyalists away from their allegiance to Congress. But it was always an uphill struggle serving in the ministry that Germain did. By 1779 he had lost the fickle confidence of both the king and the first lord, yet they kept him on, partly because Germain had become the symbol of a firm government policy, but partly also because they knew how difficult it would be to find anyone else to take up the poisoned chalice. Germain himself was only too willing to resign and eventually, four months after the surrender at Yorktown in October 1781, he was allowed to do so. Horace Walpole recorded Germain's parting shot to North: "You say I am to go, my Lord; — very well; — but why pray is your Lordship to stay?" It was a fair question, considering North's own long-standing lack of belief in the government's American policy, yet in the end academic, for the ministry had but a matter of weeks left to run.

The last of the Secretaries of State for the colonies in this period was Welbore Ellis, who thereby obtained by far his highest position after a lifetime of placemanship. George was almost certainly referring to the quality of obsequious deference when he remarked at the time of the Secretary's appointment in February 1782 that "so very proper conduct as that of Mr. Ellis I fear is only to be found in men of the last age". Horace Walpole was less complimentary and called him "Forlorn Hope Ellis". It was a harsh but accurate description of a man indeed hopelessly out of his depth. As Ellis wrote in some desperation to his under-secretary William Knox after a few days in office: "I send you some lines which I have very hastily strung together this morning for your correction & if they can be of any use for being incorporated with your own — I am a total stranger to these things & shall take it unkindly if you prefer politeness to the sincerity & assistance of a real friend and adviser in my public duty". But Ellis need not have worried. North's ministry ended the following month and with it, for the time being, another ill-fated third secretaryship.

II. analysis

"Every one who is at all acquainted with the constitution of this government must know that all warlike preparations, every military operation, and every naval equipment must be directed by a Secretary of State before they can be undertaken. Neither the Admiralty, Treasury, Ordnance, nor victualling boards can move a step without the King's command so signified".

The tone of William Knox's dictum, pronounced during the war with the American colonies, is an illuminating reminder of how little the basis of secretarial authority had changed since Braybrook's day four hundred years earlier. "The King's command so signified" has a ring of the ages about it. Indeed, the single thing that strikes one most about the history of the secretaryship in the period after the constitutional settlement of 1689 is the extent to which the personal connection with the monarch remained a dominant theme. William III's reign revealed this clearly: the Secretaries were weak precisely because the king chose to have other intimates around him. In particular, he designated the reliable William Blathwayt, secretary at war, to accompany him annually to Holland and Flanders from 1692 onwards. There Blathwayt acted in effect as William's Secretary of State, not as his private secretary, this being the prerogative of a fellow-Hollander. Blathwayt received the salary of a Secretary of State and when William was out of England was given care of the signet and took charge of the usual secretarial communications with envoys and agents abroad. In 1695 he was offered the official secretaryship but wisely turned it down, apparently because "without envy he is warmer as he is". Meanwhile the actual Secretaries in England could only resign themselves to possessing the reverse of Blathwayt's power-

145

without-responsibility. As Trumbull noted in June 1696: "I read this evening another foreign packet, which wants very little in return, since all the correspondence goes to Mr. Blathwayt". Shrewsbury especially was aware that Blathwayt's role was turning the secretaryship into an office of humiliating insignificance. In 1695 he complained that he was "as much unacquainted as any gentleman who lives in the country, having never heard otherwise than as they may do in news letters". Shrewsbury was entirely left in the dark during peace negotiations and a long time afterwards was compelled to admit to St John, then Secretary himself, that he was unaware of the substance of a certain commercial treaty with France. "Odd confession for a Secretary of State who was in office at the treaty of Ryswick" was St John's response to this revelation, understandable enough but wanting in historical insight.

St John ought perhaps to have perceived the nature of Shrewsbury's problem more clearly, for in a certain sense he himself was almost as dependent on Queen Anne as with such different effects Blathwayt and Shrewsbury had been on King William. In the early summer of 1714, for example, he lost significant ground to Harley because the queen disliked the way he had been so blatantly abusing his wife's fidelity; and in July of course Anne's death proved a hammer blow. In the years that followed, the golden secretarial rule of staying close to the first two Georges during their stays in Hanover confirmed the continuing pattern. In 1723 indeed, Townshend and Carteret both accompanied the king, each making sure that the one did not do the other down. For as Townshend reported back home: "If there be any place in the world where faction and intrigue are natural and in fashion it is here". A quarter of a century later much the same fears and suspicions still prevailed. Newcastle was no sailor even after he became Secretary, but in 1748, unwilling to give Bedford the opportunity to make some telling blows in his personal absence, he overcame his apprehension and followed the king to Hanover. Moreover, if such was the pattern under the relatively sluggish first two Georges, then the need to cling on to the royal favour was intensified under the far more involved kingship of George III, who during the 1760s made and unmade ministries with an unquestioned freedom, if by no means ease. Pitt was only reflecting the convention of the day when in 1761 he accepted without demur that the king no longer wished to have him as Secretary. The last word remained with the monarch. Where George went wrong was in so wilfully exhausting his vocabulary within a decade of coming to the throne.

For of course time had not stood still since the flight of James II. Even while the Secretaries were grumbling, the constitutional settlement had confirmed the indispensability of Parliament and the Triennial Act of 1694 further struck at court manipulation. The effect was permanent and not significantly altered by the Septennial Act of 1716. A central figure in all this was Nottingham, who on assuming the secretaryship in March 1689 informed William that, in Burnet's words, "he would follow his own sense of things in Parliament, though he would be guided by the King's sense out of it". It was a formative declaration and revealed as dead the era of Coke and Coventry. To be a responsible minister, moreover, now meant to be attached to a political party or faction, as Nottingham discovered first to his cost in 1693 when the Whigs brought him down, but then to his satisfaction when in 1702 one of the conditions on which he reassumed the secretaryship was that he be authorised to rid the local government of London of its Whig elements. Nevertheless, as the affirmation of intent to William suggests, Nottingham saw himself as much the king's executive agent as a leading minister responsible to Parliament and deriving his authority from that connection. This potential conflict was not to be decisively resolved until George III's madness a century later, though the omens were apparent from the death of William, and the intervening period is full of examples of the secretaryship in a continuing state of transition. In the 1700s, for instance, Marlborough and Godolphin were able broadly to determine foreign policy because of Anne's personal confidence in them, but they still went through the Secretaries in the everyday course of diplomacy. In the late 1740s, Pelham argued that, contrary to his brother's opinion, Bedford should be encouraged to stay in office because he would be less able to influence the king if he was still tied down by the manifold duties of his secretaryship. Perhaps most revealingly of all, Bute in 1761 decided that, despite being the king's great friend, his household offices were not sufficient to enable him to match the career politicians and that he must become Secretary as well. The secretaryship now represented high ministerial office and to be without such an office was as bad as to be without the royal confidence. Slowly, indeed, it was even becoming worse.

Continuing Versatility

It is impossible to divorce the developing ministerial status of the secretaryship from the growth in the eighteenth century of the modern cabinet. During Anne's reign the lords of the committee, in effect the cabinet, were meeting at least weekly in the secretarial office situated at the Cockpit; Newcastle under the first two Georges had himself designated as the official recorder of cabinet proceedings; and Fox, though made a member of the outer cabinet in 1754 when he was appointed secretary at war, had to wait until becoming Secretary of State the following year to join the inner cabinet, which alone signified. The Secretary's cabinet role in this period seems to have been similar to his conciliar one during the previous two centuries: namely, introducing his proposals and slanting the subsequent discussion accordingly. The familiar pitfalls remained despite the theoretical ministerial unity that the cabinet embodied. Newcastle in 1765 was drawing on personal experience when he advised the new Secretary, Conway, that "the resolution of every meeting of the King's servants should be reduced into a minute", for otherwise "there is no security for the execution of what is agreed". The Secretary, moreover, suffered from his divided authority and in general was always liable to carry less influence than the first lord of the treasury. Walpole, Pelham, and North were not only at the head of a sophisticated department increasingly in control of government patronage, but also they each made sure that the Secretaries of the day did not interfere with their personal power base in the Commons. Walpole in 1730, for example, was prepared to allow Pulteney to succeed Townshend, but only if he became a peer, which offer Pulteney sensibly declined. First lords of the treasury who were not in the Commons almost invariably found themselves in trouble as a result. It was on account of his parliamentary indispensability that St John in the first part of his secretaryship was able to wrest from Harley's hands some measure of control over the French negotiations. And in the mid-1750s the sequence of Robinson, Fox, and Pitt as Secretaries indicated the problems Newcastle faced as first lord after he had taken over the office from his brother. It only needed a forceful Secretary to bring him down and such a man was Pitt. But these were exceptional instances: very few eighteenth-century Secretaries were members of the Commons and even Pitt, though dominant there, tried later in the 1750s to establish a *modus vivendi* with Newcastle and suppress his natural instinct to conduct treasury business also. Nevertheless, the fact that the "prime ministers" of the period were usually first lords rather than Secretaries by no means meant that the eighteenth century represented lost ground for the secretaryship. In several important spheres, quite apart from matters domestic and diplomatic, the Secretaries performed a significant holding operation on the growth of other embryonic departments of government.

The army (as Knox's affirmation of the 1770s suggests) was a prime case in point. Though Blathwayt as William III's secretary at war enjoyed considerable military authority and Marlborough as commander-in-chief during the 1700s was very much his own man, the balance then changed. The secretaries at war were on the whole junior politicians, not usually as bold as the young St John; and consequently Secretaries of State were able to assert themselves, issuing the important military instructions directly via the secretaries at war, controlling army patronage, and supervising the board of ordnance. St John indeed was even more active in the military sphere after he actually became Secretary of State in 1710. The following year he dispatched what was almost a private expedition to Quebec, partly because he saw a profitable sideline in providing the soldiers with their outfits; and in 1712, while negotiations were taking place at Utrecht, he intrigued with Louis XIV in sending the infamous and probably unauthorised "orders of restraint" to Ormonde in command of the British army. Secretarial control further increased under the Hanoverians and gradually it became the accepted practice for each Secretary to be responsible for the soldiers operating in his particular province. The value of this authority varied enormously, being minimal under Newcastle, at its most productive under Pitt. The Secretaries were also still responsible for ensuring that the local lords-lieutenant kept the militia in trim and in this duty Pitt again was supreme. He put the Militia Act of 1757 into effect with great energy and demonstrated that if the right man had the job a Secretary could still defend his country's security with the wide-ranging competence inherited from William Cecil and Walsingham two centuries earlier. The military authority continued to exist in the absence of a proper war minister and the crucial question was how it was used. From Minden to Yorktown proved a hard road for Germain and he would at least have endured less vilification if he had indeed in 1759 suffered the same fate as poor Admiral Byng after the loss of Minorca and been shot.

Secretarial influence over naval matters followed a somewhat similar pattern. The key figure was Nottingham, who William realised could issue far more flexible naval orders in his capacity as Secretary than a formal body like the admiralty could hope to do. Nottingham made the most of the opportunity and issued orders both directly and through the admiralty itself. It is true that eventually he was brought down by a naval dispute and that the admiralty subsequently recovered some ground in the three years between the death of Trenchard and the end of the war, but on the whole the trend was clear. Conflict was latent in such a situation and Shrewsbury in September 1694 was compelled to write to Blathwayt that "I have so often told you that the ships were sailing or sailed upon the attempt against Dunkirk, that I am almost ashamed to repeat it". From 1708 the admiralty did secure cabinet representation, but already the tenure during the previous six years of the feeble Prince George of Denmark as lord high admiral had further strengthened the naval authority of the Secretaries when it came to taking the critical decisions. It was a measure of their established influence that when in the mid-1700s St John as secretary at war tried to impose himself, the admiralty would have none of it and continued to take instructions only from the Secretaries of State. The Secretaries themselves tended to take as much or as little interest in naval affairs as it pleased them, each being theoretically responsible for the fleets of his own province. Newcastle during the war years between 1739 and 1748 did not wish to abnegate his duties, but typically was very nervous of being laden with the blame for a naval disaster. He was well aware that ruling the waves was not his forte* and he even took his cowardice to the extent of not countersigning certain instructions. Pitt inevitably was far more dynamic. He still worked through the admiralty, but regarded it as only an administrative pawn in a much grander design that assumed the interdependence of political, military, and naval considerations. The fact that he could plan as he did as Secretary was justification perhaps for the retarded growth of executive departmentalisation.

The American war presented the other side of the coin. One of the major indirect causes of the rebellion was undoubtedly the way in which Secretaries during the eighteenth century consistently prevented the board of trade from developing after its foundation in 1696 into an autonomous department capable of giving the colonies the concentrated attention they needed. The board was set up primarily as a policy-making body, but from the outset there was no clear demarcation between the extent of its authority and that of the Secretary in the southern department. Nottingham in 1702 pointed the way by instructing colonial governors to correspond with him and not merely the board; and in 1706, after two years of friendly relations with Hedges, the board was decisively put in its place by Sunderland. His attitude was domineering from the first and, by persistently emphasising that he was entitled to see all colonial documents before they went to the queen, he soon cowed the members of the board. Typical was their response when Vetch in the summer of 1708 put forward a plan for a Canadian expedition: Sunderland was out of town at the time and the board awaited for three months before considering the plan and then deferentially submitting their approval of it to the returning Secretary. Things scarcely improved under Dartmouth, who put up little resistance when the incorrigibly aggressive St John encroached on his colonial influence and patronage. And after 1714 the board passed into a long period of virtual insignificance. Newcastle in 1724 was behaving like any other Secretary for the south when on his appointment he immediately assumed authority over the colonial governors. The only threat to Newcastle came not from the board but from Walpole at the treasury, though on the whole, certainly from the

---

*Smollett agreed. In *The Expedition of Humphrey Clinker* (1966 Oxford University Press edition, p. 111) he has one of his characters discoursing on the inadequacies of the duke: "In the beginning of the war, this poor half-witted creature told me, in a great fright, that thirty thousand French had marched from Arcadia to Cape Breton. 'Where did they find transports?' said I. 'Transports!' cried he, 'I tell you they marched by land'. 'By land to the island of Cape Breton?' 'What! is Cape Breton an island?' 'Certainly'. 'Ha! are you sure of that?' When I pointed it out in the map he examined it earnestly with his spectacles; then, taking me in his arms, 'My dear C——!' cried he, 'you always bring us good news. Egad, I'll go directly, and tell the king that Cape Breton is an island'".

1730s, he kept a reasonably complete grip on the dispensation of colonial patronage. There have been attempts to do a salvage job on this aspect of Newcastle's reputation and suggest that his all-pervasive patronage did not really depress the local authority of the colonial governors, but it is a difficult argument to sustain. In 1748, however, Newcastle moved to the northern department, and the board of trade, if not the colonial governors, came back into contention.

The same year also saw the appointment of a new president of the board, Halifax, who was determined to improve on the ineffectual performance of his predecessors and right the balance. Bedford and Holdernesse in turn in the southern department offered him relatively little opposition and even by 1750 Newcastle, asked by Pelham for an opinion on the possibility of Halifax replacing Bedford, was observing that "he is so conceited of his parts that he would not be there one month without thinking he knew as much or more of the business than any one man". It was a judicious estimate, though spoken with gall, for Newcastle two years earlier had favoured Halifax's candidature for the presidency. By 1752 Newcastle was certain of his original mistake. Halifax that year, by an order in council, acquired colonial patronage, permission to attend cabinet on colonial business, and the satisfaction of knowing that colonial governors were only to correspond with the Secretaries on specifically military or diplomatic matters. But Halifax had also pressed to be created actual Secretary for the colonies and in this respect he failed. 1752, indeed, marked the high point of the board's influence. Pitt four years later unofficially regained much colonial authority and then early in 1761, following Halifax's resignation as president, had the order of 1752 revoked. The southern Secretaries after Pitt proved to be hardly of the calibre to warrant his effort, but once more in 1766 he had Shelburne as Secretary cast into the centre of colonial affairs and Hillsborough as president of the board reduced to a cipher. The failure of this return to the traditional eighteenth-century approach to colonial affairs soon showed itself to be complete, yet when in 1768 long-overdue reorganisation did take place it was not the board of trade that was made into a separate colonial department but instead the secretaryship itself that was further divided. Hillsborough's hard line on colonial policy was at last rewarded and he assumed the new office as the king's man. Personal monarchy thus continued to the last to stall necessary administrative reforms and the secretaryship remained the Crown's chief instrument.

Foreign Concerns

In November 1756, as Fox was looking to give up the secretaryship, he received a stricture, in vain as it proved, from Carteret his mentor: "You *should* be ambitious. I want to instil a noble ambition into you; to make you knock the heads of the Kings of Europe together, and jumble something out that may be of service to this country". These words of the old Secretary testify well the extent to which the conduct of high diplomacy continued to exist at the very heart of the office. Yet as much as ever the eighteenth-century Secretary remained as a foreign minister at the mercy of the king and his fellow office-holders, to such a degree that diplomatic negotiations seldom took place in London precisely because of the likelihood of this interference. The threat stayed double-headed, for although under the early Hanoverians there did gradually take place the transition from ultimate royal control over the conduct of foreign policy to what was by the middle of the century in effect cabinet control, nevertheless the king had to be consulted before any major directive was issued. Craggs wrote to Stanhope in 1718 that George "always expresses a great deal of dislike when a post arrives without any letters"; and two years later Stanhope himself was forced to send a follow-up dispatch to Vienna, revoking previous orders to St Saphorin there, after discovering from an audience with George that the king had "quite different views on the proposals made to you from those I first conceived on reading your dispatch". The monarch continued to have an important say in the choice and location of envoys and it took Newcastle a long time to persuade George II, a latter-day Elizabeth, of the need to make provision for a minister in Berlin. George II also fought in the 1740s a stubborn and not entirely futile rearguard action to have the interests of his electorate kept as a central priority of English foreign policy. And twenty years later, of course, George III tried his hardest to use his ministries for the ends he saw fit, on one occasion, during the peace preliminaries of 1762, "speaking daggers" to the hapless but still-resisting Egremont. But in general the trend was the other way. "I think this draft very right" was a more typical Hanoverian phrase, here

used by George II in June 1730 as he minuted his approval of a
dispatch drawn up by Newcastle. If there was one decisive moment, in
terms of the first two Georges, perhaps it came in November 1743. The
king and Carteret were both in favour of the ratification of the Treaty
of Worms, but the cabinet voted eight to five against it and George
thereupon submitted with reasonably good grace. Though his grandson might subsequently deplore such surrenders, George II at least
could see on which ground it was useless to fight.

In a technical as well as a policy-making sense, the rise of the
cabinet complicated considerably the Secretary's conduct of diplomacy.
He was not only expected to read out to his fellow-members as a
subject for discussion the critical passages of dispatches received from
envoys, even supposedly "private" communications, but also to inform
them of the general drift of what he proposed as a response. Behind
the cabinet, moreover, stood Parliament and public opinion. Stanhope,
for instance, found himself almost alone in having a low opinion of the
value of retaining Gibraltar rather than Port Mahon as a base in the
Mediterranean. And increasingly Secretaries were having to produce
their diplomatic correspondence for parliamentary inspection. This
they did with the utmost reluctance, so that by 1762 there were
complaints from the opposition about "these few and scanty materials"
being "imperfect and mutilated" as well as "so sparingly dealt out to
the public". One should not, however, over-formalise the situation.
Constitutional developments leading to a more responsible form of
government took place but slowly in the eighteenth century, and the
chief threat to secretarial autonomy in the conduct of foreign policy
came much more from ambitious ministerial colleagues, especially a
succession of first lords of the treasury anxious to assert their own
authority. Sometimes the conflict had a genuine administrative basis
to it, as when Newcastle in December 1761 rebuked Bute ("My Lord,
troops are money") on hearing that the Secretary had vouchsafed
6,000 soldiers to Portugal. But more often the motivation was
transparently political, as when Walpole in 1725 advised Townshend
to cut down on the expenses of an embassy the Secretary was sending to
France or when Newcastle in 1756 wrote to Mitchell in Berlin about
the need for secrecy in their communications: "I should be most
unhappy if Lord Holdernesse should know it who might imagine that I

was sending you orders when I only mean to give you a notion of my own way of thinking". Newcastle himself as Secretary had known what it was like to be subordinate to the first lord. The king may have given his approval early in June 1730 to the Secretary's dispatch, but later in the month Newcastle revealed all when he wrote to George about a further version that had been drawn up of the same dispatch to the envoy in Madrid: "In an affair of this consequence I would not presume to lay it before your Majesty till some other of your Majesty's servants had seen it. I therefore sent it yesterday evening to Sir Robert Walpole, who has returned it this morning and is humbly of opinion, if your Majesty approves of it, that it may be very proper to be sent". It did not need the bitter struggle between Harley and St John to show that what in the end turned the scales was political rather than purely office-holding weight. And when in 1737 Newcastle was able to reject the Walpole nominee for a forthcoming mission to Naples, this was an indication far less of growing secretarial status as such than of his own new-found personal strength within the ministry. Less than twenty years on he himself would with much-practised ease be lording it over three at least of the Secretaries.

Among themselves, moreover, the Secretaries seemed to remain as conflict-ridden as ever. Though it is possible to argue that the division into provinces meant that one Secretary would always have to dominate the other if a coherent foreign policy was to emerge, this hardly justifies much of the animosity and palpable political intent that characterised the period's inter-secretarial rivalry. The prime culprit was obviously Newcastle, but he was by no means alone. One has only to go through the list of Secretaries to see what amounts to virtually a succession of antagonistic partnerships. A fairly typical episode occurred in the summer of 1762, during the bartering over peace terms. Grenville was all for holding on to Guadaloupe, or at least getting a comparable exchange for it, but unfortunately for him he took sick and Bute in his absence quickly held a cabinet meeting and obtained authorisation for the island's surrender. It is true that some Secretaries did work well together, like Stanhope and Townshend during the Jacobite rebellion of 1715, and also that the Secretaries of the period did in their run-of-the-mill diplomatic correspondence tend to respect the provincial boundaries rather more than had previously been the case. Yet there could still be muddle, as when Nottingham's report of 1693 about French activities failed to get to the English admirals because of confused relations between himself and Trenchard; while only rarely did the more powerful Secretary respect his colleague's formal authority if there was a significant issue at stake in, as it were, the junior province. The continuing habit of retiring Secretaries taking their documents with them reflected this painfully slow growth of secretarial unity. Sunderland in 1710 and Dartmouth in 1713 were but two of the offenders; and Grenville, the century's Williamson, conducted in the 1760s almost a lone campaign to do something positive about the problem. Perhaps it *was* the provincial division that lay at the root of the whole matter. After Harley in 1712 had been using Dartmouth to negotiate on his behalf with the French, which was fair enough in that Dartmouth was the Secretary for the southern department, a friend reported to the treasurer in October: "I have been this morning with my Lord Dartmouth, who tells me Lord Bolingbroke treated him last night in so rough a manner that he believes it will be impossible for you to find any expedient to keep them together". The notion that the emergence of the position of prime minister was directly related to the need to keep warring Secretaries apart is not on this evidence entirely fanciful. Nor was St John the only Secretary who thought of himself as the foreign minister, yet to his acute frustration found himself possessing only half the authority of such a minister.

Roughly one in two of the Secretaries of the period were in fact qualified for the office in terms of personal diplomatic experience. Up to 1714 and after 1760 they tended not to have had this training, but under the first two Georges the opposite usually applied, with of course the major exception of Newcastle. Both kings admired professionalism and George II was particularly vexed when the death of Pelham indirectly forced him (after Robinson's unhappy tenure) to accept first Fox and then Pitt primarily as political figures capable of filling the vacuum in the Commons. As he had bluntly observed to Fox about Pitt, with of course no idea of how well things would turn out: "What a strange country is this! I have never known but two or three men in it who understood foreign affairs: you do not study them — and yet here comes one man, and says he has not so much as read Wicquefort, has

all to learn, and demands to be Secretary of State!" Though the
grievance was theoretically a good one, things were in fact to get much
worse under his grandson, who chose Secretaries who were not only
ill-qualified but also very often political nonentities. Suffolk, unable to
speak French, perhaps represented the nadir. But the trend away from
qualified diplomatists was probably inevitable, granted the increasingly
political nature of the major offices in general as well as the gradual
subterranean development of a permanent civil service. Chesterfield
even under George II perceived this non-meritocratic core of the
situation when he wrote in one of his *Letters to his Son:* "If to your
merit and knowledge, you add the art of pleasing, you may very
probably come in time to be Secretary of State; but, take my word for
it, twice your merit and knowledge, without the art of pleasing, would
at most raise you to the *important post* of Resident at Hamburg or
Ratisbon". "Pleasing" meant different things to different kings, but
the burden of Chesterfield's irony was clear. In a sense, moreover,
George III was no more than the governing class deserved. The young
Jenkinson spent some time learning the ropes in Holdernesse's office,
but in 1758 felt compelled to record that "though the English are very
great politicians, they have, I believe, fewer books on public law or
anything that relates to foreign policy than any other nation in the
world". It is a sobering point and suggests a framework within which
the generally ill-treated diplomatic corps of the eighteenth century is
readily set.

The complaints from abroad had the usual tone about them: "A
single word gives sometimes more light than twenty dispatches of
state", wrote Robinson in Vienna to Newcastle's private secretary,
Andrew Stone. And on another occasion Robinson observed still more
gloomily to a fellow-envoy: "I expect nothing from England till the
opening of the Parliament when I shall take the King's speech as my
clue for the ensuing year". Such a lack of secretarial guidance is
especially shameful when one considers how unattractive the career of
a diplomatist was. Rank rather than duties continued to determine the
allowance he received and often it was very difficult to fill vacant
positions. As Horace Walpole noted in 1766: "Sir James Gray goes to
Madrid. The embassy has been sadly hawked about; not a peer that
would take it". Possibly the diplomatic service was beginning to attain

a degree of professionalism which it had not had previously, but on the whole one is struck by how haphazard the process of diplomacy remained. In 1735 Lord Kinnoull, a most perverse character, actually refused orders for his recall and stayed on making trouble at Constantinople for a year beyond his time even after Newcastle had sent out a man-of-war to try and bring him back. It is true that in 1724 George I did found chairs of modern history at Oxford and Cambridge in order to provide the historical and linguistic training necessary to build up a qualified corps of diplomatists, but the attempt came to practically nothing because both Townshend and Newcastle preferred to fill the junior positions in their offices with young men who had something politically more tangible to offer than a degree in modern history. Connection remained dominant and the professorships at the universities soon became the sinecure reminders of another defeat for German professionalism.

To a remarkable extent, indeed, old-fashioned questions of communications, security, and intelligence continued for a long time to preoccupy the Secretaries in their approach to foreign affairs. Even when circumstances were propitious, it took about three weeks for a dispatch to get to Rome or Madrid, close on seven to reach Constantinople. It must have been a fraught business and it was perhaps significant when in 1772 the Secretaries took over control from the lord chamberlain of 16 of the government's full-time messengers. Matters were not helped by the fact that the cost of constructing a new cipher was well over £100 and that as a result old ciphers were often retained too long and used too widely. The fear of interception and revelation naturally still loomed large in the secretarial mind, as when Shrewsbury in 1695 rebuked Admiral Russell for sending a letter through France "that gave so exact an account of the condition of your fleet, and how it was to be disposed of the rest of the summer". Trenchard's instincts had been similarly traditional two years earlier when, after assuming the secretaryship, he almost at once turned his attention to the problem of getting the spy network functioning properly in the major French ports. Almost half a century later little had changed, for Newcastle appears to have spent a disproportionate amount of his time going through secret service reports. Typical of his rooted attitudes was his desire during the War of the Austrian Succession to have large and heavily-defended packet-boats carrying the mails. In this he was at odds with Pelham, who followed William III's example and successfully insisted on smaller and therefore speedier vessels. Not until the end of the Jacobite threat and the years of peace on either side of the Seven Years War did the acquisition of secret intelligence significantly recede as a central secretarial pursuit. By 1779, indeed, concern had so declined that Stormont was forced to point out to George III that "there is at present a want of regular, immediate, secret intelligence that is highly prejudicial to your Majesty's service". It was possibly a fair enough point to make at the particular time, yet in the long-term sense it is doubtful whether the yield of prime intelligence from abroad had ever since Walsingham's day justified the outlay of expenditure, time, and sheer muddled anxiety. The nature of diplomacy itself was changing, but the Secretaries themselves hardly seemed to realise that their role must change accordingly. As in so many respects the disastrous course of the American war provided the most salutary of lessons.

Secretarial in-fighting during the 1770s, and in particular the troubled history of the colonial secretaryship, proved in several ways an appropriate finale to the conduct of foreign affairs during the period. It is perhaps worth quoting the preamble to the patent appointing Hillsborough as Secretary in 1768: "Whereas the business of our Colonies and Plantations increasing, it seemeth expedient to us to appoint one other Principal Secretary of State besides our two ancient Secretaries". Hillsborough's status thus appeared to be clear, but in the actual exercise of his authority he soon found himself coming under pressure from his fellow-Secretaries, especially in connection with the control of troops and ships in the colonial sphere. Hillsborough just about held his own, but the bitterness caused by this new provincial division within the secretaryship, made all the greater by the political prominence of the colonial question, inevitably hindered the execution of a unified policy. Suffolk in particular, though the northern Secretary, viewed the colonies as part of the traditional concerns of the "ancient" Secretaries and, following Hillsborough's resignation, gave Dartmouth an extremely rough passage. The test-case, however, came when the more assertive Germain succeeded Dartmouth in November 1775 and both Suffolk and Weymouth contended that the third secretaryship was a new office, which therefore under the terms of Queen Anne's Place Acts made Germain ineligible. The intention was clearly to put the third secretaryship on a footing below that of the two older ones, but George would have none of it. In front of the privy council, including the two new Secretaries, Weymouth and Germain, he declared that "there are two Secretaries of State, let them both be sworn together". It was a princely gesture and confirmed the theoretical indivisibility of the secretaryship. Germain was now able not only to be known as "One of His Majesty's Principal Secretaries of State", but also to assert his authority in the colonial sphere in which it was tacitly recognised his responsibilities lay. Yet not until the provincial division itself was abolished could interminable departmental squabbling over foreign matters cease. That major step awaited the aftermath rather than the anticipation of the American war and at the same time ended the inner history of the office. The notion of the omnicompetent Secretary had been traditional and remarkable, but it had also shown itself during the eighteenth century to be increasingly an administrative liability, apart perhaps from Pitt's tenure, and was now at long last considered dispensable.

Domestic Concerns

Domestic affairs tended in secretarial eyes to be appreciably less important than foreign, but again the acquisition of intelligence remained significant, if no longer as central a concern as before. In his memorandum of March 1689 to Nottingham about secretarial procedure, Sir Robert Southwell (who the following year accompanied William to Ireland) advised the new Secretary "to think of spies and intelligence, where needful abroad; and the like more especially at home, in several parts of the kingdom, and in particular to know what passes in London and at the Exchange". The most able Secretary of the period in these obscure pathways was probably Harley, whose domestic intelligence enabled him in 1705 to forecast accurately and in detail the election results of that year. Over the next two years he spent much time planting suitable agents in Scotland to get the union through and during this phase made perceptive use of the services of Defoe both as an informer and propagandist. The Secretaries continued of course, like Thomas Cromwell two centuries earlier, to receive a fair amount of gentry correspondence relating to matters of internal security. During the Gordon Riots of 1780, for example, Hillsborough heard from a correspondent in Alton that "when the unhappy commotions in London reached the country, the lower class of the people seemed inclineable to join them". On the whole, however, it was now less by paid informers or deliberate correspondents, and much more by the systematic interception of postal communications, that the Secretaries were able to keep tabs on potentially subversive activities. The Post Office Act of 1711 confirmed that they alone were entitled to authorise the opening of letters and under their auspices the private office dealt with the inland correspondence, leaving the secret office to sift through communications either from or to foreign representatives based in England. The consequences of the work undertaken in the private office were inevitably diverse and ranged from the enforced exile of Atterbury in 1723 on account of his Jacobite correspondence to the revelation in 1757 that the financier Vanneck had been putting his money into enemy securities. The office was allowed during this period to get on quietly with its work, apart from two ineffectual attempts by the Commons to inquire into the practice of interception. In other, more exposed areas of their domestic prerogative, however, the Secretaries found themselves being visibly and rudely cut back.

The two principal issues at stake concerned the quelling of public disturbances and the issuing of general warrants. Though the absence of a police system meant that as in previous centuries the burden of keeping the daily peace fell on the ill-equipped local authorities, nevertheless the Secretaries were on occasion compelled to intervene personally and authorise the use of the military. Sunderland during Sacheverell's trial in 1710 deployed the Guards in order to disperse rioting Londoners and defend government strongholds; and Newcastle as Secretary does not seem to have hesitated to send in troops to put down bouts of local disaffection. In 1769, however, serious criticism was voiced after the bloody suppression of a riot in St George's Fields had followed Weymouth's confident declaration to the chairman of the Southwark Quarter Sessions that the military could have no "more constitutional purpose than in support of the authority and dignity of the magistracy". Burke among others denied the claim and asserted in the Commons that "the military power cannot be employed to any constitutional purpose whatever". Burke did not mention the lack of an ultimate alternative as far as the Secretary was concerned to that of sending in the troops in order to maintain the peace, but the criticism itself told and both Stormont and Hillsborough moved gingerly during the Gordon Riots a decade later. A much more serious blow at the time, however, to discretionary secretarial authority was the attack already launched on their use of general warrants, which in practice had not been terminated by the expiry of the Licensing Act in 1695. Inevitably the figure at the centre of the storm was John Wilkes, who in 1763 was, as a prime suspect, arrested with 48 other people in connection with libellous anti-government writings in issue number 45 of the *North Briton*. Wilkes also had his papers seized and the whole episode initiated three set-piece legal examinations concerning the scope of the secretarial authority.

The first involved Wilkes himself. *Wilkes* v. *Wood* took place in 1763 in front of the Court of Common Pleas and the hapless defendant was Egremont's under-secretary, even though Halifax and his under-secretary had been far more involved in the issuing of the various general warrants. Pratt the judge ruled against the secretarial action of seizing Wilkes's papers and Wilkes himself received £1,000 in damages. Two years later the case of *Entick* v. *Carrington*, again in front of Pratt, now Lord Camden, confirmed the limitation. Entick was a freelance journalist, Carrington one of four royal messengers who had seized his papers, using as their authority a general warrant signed by Halifax in 1762. Camden during the case considered the nature of the secretaryship. He observed that the position had evolved into a leading ministerial office only because the "whole foreign correspondence passed through the Secretary's hands". And he went on: "This being the true description of his employment, I see no part of it that requires the authority of a magistrate". It was a point-scoring argument, complete with phrases like "subversive of all the comforts of society" to describe the seizing of papers, and Entick duly received damages. Even more important, however, was the case the same year in front of the King's Bench of *Leach* v. *Money*, which settled that Secretaries could not use general warrants to bring in on nebulous charges a haul of assorted suspects from which the guilty could then be weeded out. Leach was in fact a printer who had been imprisoned at the time of issue number 45 of the *North Briton* and Money once again one of the three king's messengers who had actually done the dirty work of physical seizure. As it turned out, the secretarial humiliation was compounded by the revelation that Leach had had nothing to do with the particular issue of the paper. Justice Mansfield proved less harsh on the Secretaries than Camden, but nevertheless condemned to oblivion the practice of issuing general warrants without naming the persons to be arrested when he described it as not a general usage according to accepted custom, but instead "only the usage of a particular office and contrary to the usages of all other justices and conservators of the peace". Ten years later the point came home to Rochford as a result of his folly concerning Sayn. The eighteenth century had become the age of separated powers and the memory of even a Stanhope, simultaneously in 1715 examining a treason suspect and taking part in an adjacent council meeting, let alone of a Cromwell or a Walsingham, would soon be of historical interest only.

The Man and the Office

Wood's invidious situation in 1763 was indicative of the increasing responsibility which under-secretaries of the period were bearing. Stalwarts like Fraser and Porten were by the 1770s staying immovably in their departments, northern and southern respectively, whoever the actual Secretaries of State might be in the political overworld. Most new Secretaries retained the existing secretarial staff, which by the end of the period was receiving a regular fixed income out of Post Office funds. The Secretaries themselves often came to rely heavily on the two under-secretaries they each had. Carteret, for example, provided general guidance, but was almost entirely dependent on Weston for getting through the routine correspondence; while Suffolk typically complained to Eden with great feebleness that "you leave the labouring oar too much upon me". One of the most able and therefore influential of under-secretaries was Knox in the colonial department. George III praised him in 1776 for "that precision which it would be no disadvantage to other departments if they would imitate" and Germain gave him partridges in gratitude for only being required to concern himself with, in Knox's words, "capital leading cases". The under-secretaries, however, by no means had the field completely to themselves. Though they were the clear forerunners of the nineteenth-century permanent bureaucracy, nevertheless Secretaries of State could still use their own private secretaries in a highly significant way. Newcastle in 1748, for instance, first sent Stone to watch over George in Hanover before he finally departed himself. But perhaps the most notable episode concerned Pitt, engaged in his house in St James's Square in a policy dispute with various of his colleagues, turning to Francis his young amenuensis, taking notes, to help him answer their criticisms. Francis subsequently recalled what occurred: "Pitt replied passionately: 'My Lords, the reasons why I consider the measure injudicious are so obvious that I wonder you should be required to be told them. I will venture to assert they will occur to that youth. Speak, Francis: have you heard the question?' 'Yes, Sir'. 'Then tell their Lordships why I object to their proposals'. It was an awful moment, but I gave an instant reason, on which Pitt, pleased, said, 'I told you how it would be: you cannot answer a boy'". William Cecil's hop-pole analogy still had a little mileage left in it yet.

Indeed, the personal connection between Secretary and secretariat remained almost as hardy in the eighteenth century as that between monarch and Secretary. Secretaries tended to stay in the same office even when they changed departments and they alone had the final responsibility for appointing, subsidising, and dismissing members of their staff. This contributed heavily to the failure of the central executive during the period to achieve the administrative autonomy earlier suggested by a figure like Williamson. Shelburne's southern department may in 1768 have had four clerks in it who totalled sixty-three years of experience between them, but equally revealing was the succession of seven under-secretaries in the colonial department in a space of only fourteen years. Under-secretaries were still liable to be factionally-minded and the ones in the colonial department, Knox included, were loud in their complaints about Eden's activities on behalf of Suffolk and the illegitimate colonial influence of the southern department. Shelburne did try to get his staff paid adequately and therefore be less dependent on fees and his own pocket, but the treasury, though it subsidised almost every department, declined to do likewise on behalf of the Secretaries. The consequences of this continuing personal attachment and absence of a decent salary, even after the Post Office's grant, can only have been harmful to the efficient working of the secretariat. As Defoe noted in relation to the early 1700s: "I have been in the Secretary's office of a post night, when had I been a French spy I could have put in my pocket my Lord Nottingham's letters directed to Sir George Rooke and to the Duke of Marlborough, laid carelessly on the table for the doorkeeper to carry to the post office". Moreover, it is probable that most Secretaries felt empowered to abuse their staff freely, to judge by Dartmouth's "one great defect" apparently being, according to Swift in 1711, that "he treats his clerks with more civility and good manners than others in his station have done the queen". The scorn was evident, as half a century later Charles Brietzcke, a clerk in the Secretary's office from 1756 to 1795, amply recorded in his diary for the early 1760s. On 15th January 1761 matters seemed fine: "At the office evg. & as I thought everything was come from my Lord went home". But on the next day came the reckoning: "Hear I was asked for last night as soon as I was gone, tho' I waited till the box came from my Lds. Upon my word, it is impossible to do anything in order till the head (my Lord Holdernesse) will be so himself". And Brietzcke was moved to add: "My Lord set out this mg. for Yorkshire to be present at the meeting & I don't care if he never returns". Yet there was perhaps a touch of false bravado about this heartfelt wish. Secretariats could still not function very long without the personal presence of the Secretary himself. The colonial department was probably more efficient during the 1770s than the other two, but even so one of the under-secretaries, Pownall, was forced to admit during a gap between Secretaries that matters consequently unattended had piled up to such an extent that, as he said, "I tremble to look at it". Brietzcke perhaps wished it otherwise, but the relationship between the Secretary and his staff was still at root symbiotic.

As ever one returns to the personal element. "Even when things go best, it has its disgusts" is an aphorism about being Secretary that might have been coined at almost any time, but in fact was enunciated by Shrewsbury in the 1690s. The secretaryship did of course become more political in the course of the eighteenth century, yet never did the quality of the holder become a less important consideration than the fact of the office. Newcastle's extremely long tenure, despite his far from outstanding talents, came close to proving the exception, but even he was usually energetic and hard-working. Indeed, it is the time-honoured theme of secretarial toil, even in this notoriously indolent period, which one should perhaps end by recalling. Johnson may have given the secretaryship a bad name by rebuking Chesterfield for his tardy patronage, but Addison on behalf of the poets had already discovered that the Secretary also could be a lonely and ill-considered figure at the desk. He attended cabinet for the first time on 21st April 1717 and this was the list of things to be done that he brought away with him:

"Copy of the manifesto published at Paris for the K of F, directed to procure.

To speak to the Count de la Perouse of the protestants in the valley of Pragelas.

D'ayrolles may compliment the King of Sicily at P____ & c.

If the Bp. comes with a small retinue to Col. Stanhope show civilities & watch his motions.

Mr. Bubb to have his letters of revocation but desired not to make use of them.

Ld. Stair to observe the motions of the court.

Mr. Tunstall in the Marshalsea to be put into the hands of Squire the messenger at Ld. Parker's request.

Carnegy at Duke of Roxburgh's."

"An infinite sphere whose centre is everywhere, whose circumference is nowhere", wrote Pascal once about nature and in that same self-defining pattern, from Braybrook to Addison and beyond, lay the essence of secretarial history too.

Postscript: 1782 and After

"A thought has occurred to me . . . whether Lord Rochford could not transact the whole department of Foreign Affairs which is the case at every other Court and then Lord Suffolk might have the home departments".

T HIS proposal by George III, made to North in 1771 on account of Suffolk's linguistic deficiencies, in the event fell through. It is unlikely that North in particular was at all keen on the idea of having a colleague in complete charge of foreign affairs. Halifax in fact assumed the secretaryship in the northern department and was succeeded a few months later by Suffolk himself. But the idea lingered, in George III's mind at least, and in March 1782, on the fall of North's ministry, actually came into effect. Under Shelburne and Charles James Fox respectively, the northern department took over responsibility for foreign affairs and the southern department assumed control over domestic and colonial matters. As a peer, Shelburne acquired for the office of Home Secretary a permanent precedence (of a ceremonial kind) over that of Foreign Secretary. Contemporaries seem to have barely taken note of the change, which was not the subject of legislation, but instead was simply announced by Fox in a circular to envoys abroad after he had taken office. The low-profile tone of the change, though typical of the eighteenth century's general lack of concern about administrative efficiency, disguised its major importance. The provincial division had proved wearisome in the extreme and with its abolition a unified foreign policy under the formal authority of one minister became a possibility at least.

The other significant secretarial change in 1782 was less sensible.

167

This was the abolition of the colonial department, one of the "economical reforms" introduced by Burke during Rockingham's ministry. The American war had inevitably attached a certain stigma to the department and it proved an easy target. The reform was, however, misguided thinking on Burke's part, for the subsequent manifold increase in government business, and not just in the colonial field, could not help but mean the creation of new secretarial departments to accommodate it. This growth was at first fairly slow and usually dependent upon specific contingencies. In 1794 there was appointed a Secretary of State for war to meet the demands of the conflict with France; and in 1801 colonial responsibilities were added to the office. There the situation remained until the 1850s. In 1854 the Crimean War prompted the re-creation of a secretaryship for colonial affairs alone, thereby allowing the war office to develop separately without any colonial duties to encumber it. Four years later, following the Indian Mutiny of 1857, there was brought into being the office of Secretary of State for India. Another longish pause then followed. Already, however, Pitt the younger in 1797 had confirmed without serious opposition the principle of the theoretical indivisibility of the secretaryship. He stressed that being in possession of the seals was what defined the office in a constitutional sense and that only afterwards was the Secretary "placed in that department of business which his Majesty thinks fit to allot for him". Though it gave prime ministers a certain flexibility in being able to treat the secretaryship as one office, the concept meant little in practice. Indeed, it was precisely because of the office's increasingly divisible characteristics that the formative change of 1782 into Home and Foreign Secretaries had at long last taken place.

The real proliferation, however, has awaited the twentieth century, when so many Secretaries of State with different areas of responsibility have been created that the office itself has almost completely lost its last vestiges of meaning. After early resistance to promoting the ministers for trade and education into Secretaries of State, on the grounds that this would reduce inner-cabinet coherence, the first of the new creations took place at the end of the Great War when Winston Churchill became Secretary of State for air. Since then the rate has steadily increased: two new secretaryships between 1920 and

1945, one between 1945 and 1959, seven during the 1960s, and eight already since 1970. Mergers and abolitions have also occurred, but by the beginning of 1976, some twenty years after the formulation of Parkinson's Law, there existed no less than fourteen Secretaries of State, responsible for such diverse matters as energy, the environment, and even prices and consumer protection. It had certainly been a long and winding road from the signet seal to the supermarket.

Bibliography

There are four indispensable works:

Florence M. Greir Evans (Mrs. C. S. S. Higham): *The Principal Secretary of State: A Survey of the Office from 1558 to 1680* (1923).

J. Otway-Ruthven, *The King's Secretary and the Signet Office in the XV Century* (1939).

J. C. Sainty, *Officials of the Secretaries of State, 1660-1782* (1973).

Mark A. Thomson, *The Secretaries of State, 1681-1782* (1932).

Studies of individual Secretaries include:

Stanley Ayling, *The elder Pitt, Earl of Chatham* (1976).

Violet Barbour, *Henry Bennet, Earl of Arlington* (1914).

G. S. Brown, *The American Secretary: Colonial policy of Lord George Germain, 1775-78* (1963).

Reed Browning, *The Duke of Newcastle* (1975).

Algernon Cecil, *A Life of Robert Cecil* (1915).

Mary Dewar, *Sir Thomas Smith* (1964).

H. T. Dickinson, *Bolingbroke* (1970).

F. G. Emmison, *Tudor Secretary: Sir William Petre at Court and Home* (1961).

S. R. Gammon, *Statesman and Schemer: William, first Lord Paget, Tudor minister* (1973).

P. M. Handover, *The Second Cecil* (1959).

Henry Horwitz, *Revolution Politicks: The career of Daniel Finch, second Earl of Nottingham* (1968).

George Hilton Jones, *Charles Middleton* (1967).

Arnold Judd, *The Life of Thomas Bekynton* (1961).

J. P. Kenyon, *Robert Spencer, Earl of Sunderland* (1958).

Angus McInnes, *Robert Harley, Puritan politician* (1970).

R. B. Merriman, *Life and Letters of Thomas Cromwell*, 2 vols. (1902).

James Arthur Muller, *Stephen Gardiner and the Tudor Reaction* (1926).

Donald Nicholas, *Mr. Secretary Nicholas* (1955).

John M. Norris, *Shelburne and Reform* (1963).

Conyers Read, *Mr. Secretary Cecil and Queen Elizabeth* (1955).

Conyers Read, *Mr. Secretary Walsingham and the Policy of Queen Elizabeth*, 3 vols. (1925).

Conyers Read, *Lord Burghley and Queen Elizabeth* (1960).

Arthur Joseph Slavin, *Politics and Profit: A Study of Sir Ralph Sadler, 1507-47* (1966).

Peter Smithers, *The life of Joseph Addison* (1954).

Dorothy H. Somerville, *The King of Hearts: Charles Talbot, Duke of Shrewsbury* (1962).

Jervis Wegg, *Richard Pace, a Tudor diplomatist* (1932).

Basil Williams, *Carteret and Newcastle* (1943).

Basil Williams, *Stanhope* (1932).

Basil Williams, *The Life of William Pitt, Earl of Chatham*, 2 vols. (1913).

N.B. The biography of Walsingham by Conyers Read includes the text of Beale's treatise.

Related works:

G. E. Aylmer, *The King's Servants: the civil service of Charles I, 1625-42* (1961).

G. E. Aylmer, *The State's Servants: the civil service of the English Republic, 1649-60* (1973).

S. B. Chrimes, *An Introduction to the Administrative History of Mediaeval England* (1952).

K. L. Ellis, *The Post Office in the eighteenth Century* (1958).

G. R. Elton, *Policy and Police* (1972).

G. R. Elton, *Studies in Tudor and Stuart Politics and Government*, 2 vols. (1974).

G. R. Elton (ed.), *The Tudor Constitution* (1960).

G. R. Elton, *The Tudor Revolution in Government* (1953).

Peter Fraser, *The Intelligence of the Secretaries of State & Their Monopoly of Licensed News, 1660-88* (1956).

D. B. Horn, *The British Diplomatic Service, 1689-1789* (1961).

Michael Kammen, *A rope of sand: the colonial agents, British politics, & the American revolution* (1968).

J. P. Kenyon (ed.), *The Stuart Constitution* (1966).

P. S. Lachs, *The diplomatic corps under Charles II & James II* (1966).

Public Record Office Handbooks, No. 1, *A Guide to Seals in the Public Record Office* (1968).

Patrick Riley, *The English ministers and Scotland, 1707-27* (1964).

T. F. Tout, *Chapters in the Administrative History of Medieval England*, vol. V (1930).

Essays and Articles:

Arthur H. Basye, 'The Secretary of State for the Colonies', in *American Historical Review* (1922-3).

K. L. Ellis, 'British Communication and Diplomacy in the Eighteenth Century', in *Bulletin of the Institute of Historical Research* (1958).

George H. Guttridge, 'Lord George Germain in Office', in *American Historical Review* (1927-8).

Florence M. G. Higham (née Evans), 'A Note on the Pre-Tudor Secretary', in ed.
    A. G. Little and F. M. Powicke, *Essays in Medieval History Presented to Thomas
    Frederick Tout* (1925).
D. B. Horn, 'The Diplomatic Experience of Secretaries of State, 1660-1852', in
    History (1956).
D. B. Horn, 'The Machinery for the Conduct of British Foreign Policy in the
    Eighteenth Century', in *Journal of the Society of Archivists* (1967).
Charles Hughes, 'Nicholas Faunt's Discourse Touching the Office of Principal
    Secretary of Estate, & c., 1592', in *English Historical Review* (1905).
R. A. Preston, 'William Blathwayt and the Evolution of a Royal Personal Secretariat',
    in *History* (1949).
R. B. Wernham, 'The Disgrace of William Davison', in *English Historical Review*
    (1931).
Franklin B. Wickwire, 'King's Friends, Civil Servants, or Politicians', in *American
    Historical Review* (1965-6).

Index

174